Homeward

how one woman embraced being lost to find her way home

LAURA PARROTT PERRY

Foreword by Matt Bays

More Praise for Homeward

"HOMEWARD is a beautiful, painful, hopeful story of what we gain when all is lost. In walking home to herself–finding her own safety, healing, and rebirth–Laura Parrott Perry shares her poignant account of the greatest love story there is: falling in love with the truth of ourselves."

-Glennon Doyle, author of #1 *New York Times* Bestseller UNTAMED, founder of Together Rising

"It is rare that I stop reading a book in the middle to track down the author online and beg for her cell number so I can tell her how beautiful, honest, and breathtaking her writing is, how much it is impacting me, how special a gift she is. And now you know the story of how I have Laura's cell."

-Jen Hatmaker, New York Times bestselling-author of *Fierce, Free, and Full of Fire*, host of award-winning *For the Love* podcast, co-founder Legacy Collective

"Homeward is not a mere book; it is an invitation to live, extended from the hand of a brave writer to the heart of a weary reader. Laura Parrott Perry's refreshing honesty, unifying humor, and captivating stories, offer proof that healing has no timeline, self-compassion is a salve, and grace is ever-present. Those with hidden scars and abandoned dreams will find themselves ushered into these pages by a most welcoming and "been there" host, and they will come to know peace in their bones."

-Rachel Macy Stafford, New York Times bestselling-author, speaker, and certified special education teacher

------

"*Homeward* by Laura Parrott Perry begins with a loss described so vividly that the reader is immediately invested. Then, with care, honesty, and a quick and ready wit, Perry walks us through how she survived that time (sometimes even when she didn't want to) and how, through sobriety, friendship, and her dog, Scout, she came to re-envision her life-long search for the peace and safety of home. This book will break your heart and put it back together again in a better, more hopeful shape."

-Jessica Kantrowitz, author of *The Long Night*, *365 Days of Peace*, and *Blessings for the Long Night*

"Laura Parrott Perry writes her most recent memoir *Homeward* with the glorious emotional confidence and precision of a woman who understands that her stunning command of the English language is as much a gift to her readers as is the story herself. Laura is relentlessly truthful and so generous with her vulnerability and pain that a reader is assured that the inevitable adoration of her as our protagonist will not be misplaced. As a trauma therapist who specializes in grief and loss, I am so grateful to Laura for giving us Homeward, a story of endings and beginnings, abandonment and reclamation – but most importantly where hope and love win the day. I am a better therapist, human, and griever, for having read this gorgeous writer's work."

-Meghan Riordan Jarvis, MA, LCSW, Host of the *Grief is my Side Hustle* podcast

"The best written words are ones that help you find yourself in the margins. The ones that pierce something so true inside, you irrevocably spill over. Laura Parrott Perry is masterful at this.

Laura's latest offering, *Homeward: How one woman embraced being lost to find her way home*, recounts the devastating loss of love, home, and family. She achingly takes us through the gutting of both a present and a future, with detours into an often tumultuous past. As her life was ripped out from under her, she paid reverent attention at every turn, never once looking away. Her courage is our gain. This book is a gift.

Laura's bravery in the face of fear, coupled with exquisite writing and breathtaking insight, is a field guide for anyone who has had to dismantle a life, and raze the surrounding dreams. Or, anyone who longs to make a new life out of truth, grace, humor, and a deep love of self."

-Kate Mapother, author of the poetry collections *Tell Me You Hear the Riot* and *c a r v e d.*

"There is so much wisdom, pain, and love in *Homeward*. I found myself highlighting passages, making notes and tabbing pages so I could return to the nuggets of comfort, understanding, and humor this book is peppered with.

Fans of Glennon Doyle, Jen Hatmaker, and Elizabeth Gilbert will have a new favorite in Laura Parrott Perry. Her lyrical prose, searing honesty, and brave truth-telling create a treatise on what it means to be lost and found, to yearn for a place you've never been.

This beautiful book is more than the sum of its parts. Each essay is a stand alone gem, an exploration of some aspect of feeling alone and untethered in the world. As a whole, it's an inspiring and deeply insightful look at what makes us feel safe, and the work we have to do to find the home we were meant to have."

Julianna Miner
Author of *Raising A Screen Smart Kid: Embrace the Good and Avoid the Bad in the Digital Age*

———

"Laura and I shared our first home; we were both born in Mount Auburn Hospital in Cambridge, Massachusetts, years apart. In subsequent homes, Laura learned of peeling-paint poverty, childhood trauma, love lost and won, and courageous recovery. The home is a psychological thing for a woman. Laura gets this. The wood and bricks that hold us we decorate with our lives. With exquisite prose and a wry smile, Laura takes the reader home to heal. She invites us to be home, and at home, with self."

-Alicia B. Bridgeland, PsyD, Clinical Psychologist

———

"Laura is the kind of writer who writes brilliantly but without screaming, "Look at how finely crafted that sentence is, how perfect that image is, how compelling that turn of phrase." Her writing is all of that, but somehow reading her words mostly feels like sitting down with an old friend who's honest and wise and funny and hearing her stories and seeing yourself in them, and along the way healing some of the cracks in your own heart as she takes you on the journey to heal hers.

As soon as I started reading "Homeward" I began a list of people I wanted to share it with. Because this is a book for anyone who's ever had a relationship fall apart, and who's trying to put their life back together. It's for anyone who's doing life while also trying to remain sober (whatever your drug of choice) and walking/stumbling/

fumbling through recovery. It's for anyone well acquainted with shame, as in, shame is your little friend that goes everywhere with you, a friend who's a total A-hole, but they're your A-hole, you know? It's for anyone who knows how to look like "Everything's fine," "I'm good," "Couldn't be better" even when there's a tsunami-level shitstorm raging inside you. It's for anyone who might have just the tiniest little control issues. It's for anyone who's a virtuoso at playing small. And it's for anyone who's looking to fill that home-shaped hole inside of them. So yeah, it's for pretty much every one of us.

I'm so glad I read it. Believe me, I'll be sending a copy to almost everyone I know."

Lenora Rand
Co-founder of The Plural Guild, lyric and liturgy writer for
The Many

Author's Note

This is my story. Any time I read a memoir I'm keenly aware that it's 30 minutes of an hour-long movie. There are others who lived this story alongside me who no doubt have their own perspectives, recollections, and pain. I worked hard to discern what was my story to tell and what was not, and to come at the endeavor from a place of honesty, vulnerability, and generosity.

Glennon Doyle says "Be brave enough to tell your story and kind enough not to tell anyone else's."

Yes.

Anne Lamott wrote, "You own everything that happened to you. Tell your stories. If people wanted you to write warmly about them, they should have behaved better."

Also, yes.

Somewhere, between those two paths is a field. Come meet me there.

"This place where you are right now
God circled on a map for you."
Hafiz

For me.

Foreword
By Matt Bays

At this very moment, I am sitting in my home. It's a new home. New to me. It's the nicest house I have ever lived in, by a mile.

I recently got married to a man. Because I'm gay. I didn't know it for a very long time, but then came to terms with it over the course of thirty or so years. (I'm a quick study.) And this new marriage is how I arrived at this real nice house. I feel "at home" here. And I'm grateful.

The last time I wrote a foreword for a book, I was sitting on a couch in a different new home. It was my little baby house; real cheap and I couldn't have loved it more. I remember buying a sign for my front door that said something I can't recall. It was one of those little crafty-ass signs that said something about home. I'm not one for the kind of Mayberry cliches you find on every endcap at Hobby Lobby, but when I saw this particular sign at a farmer's market, I had an emotional moment—a realization that after many years, I had laid claim to my life. Driven a stake into my heart and made it my home, finally.

As soon as I moved into my little home, I bought brightly-colored furniture to put inside it. I covered every wall with a fresh coat of paint and tore up the carpet. I dragged bushes out of the ground with my neighbor's good ol' boy truck and painted the outside the deepest shade of navy blue you've ever seen. It was the cutest house on the street.

At last, I had arrived at being me—living authentically—for the very first time.

Both homes I've mentioned wrapped themselves around me. I expected they would make me whole. And in this way, I suppose both have let me down. Because no place of stone or wood, no matter how beautiful, has all that we need. This sacred truth is something I learned while reading the book you're holding in your hands; that being *at* home is altogether different than being *home*.

I met Laura Parrott Perry in the comments section of a blog post she'd written about coming to terms with sexual abuse. Ten thousand phone calls later, she would give the toast at my wedding. She isn't just a friend. She is a fellow traveler, confidant, source of great wisdom—a sister. She is as tested a person as I've ever known. A survivor, though not in that Destiny's Child way. She wasn't dancing her way through life. Too often, she was bearing it. Broken bones in her soul that would need to be set before they could heal. And this woman I know and love was both patient and physician. It's why I trust her. It's why you should too.

In HOMEWARD, Laura visits the homes of her past—what was and wasn't home about them. She has mud on her face from so many backyards she's been digging in. As a child, she must've howled at the moon in them. And I imagine the moon followed her around like a puppy—wondering at all she kept discovering about life. When I consider what she has endured, I wonder how there is any gravity left within her at all. How is she still here? Surely, she should be floating for all she has cast off. Should be flying or lighting up the sky. But instead, she is with us. Thank God for that.

I've seen the mud caked thick upon her, and watched as she scrubbed it clean with so much grit, with so much grace. And I marvel (like the moon, I suppose) that behind all of that mud is a knowing set of eyes, and a wisdom that gently explains the process—that fills in the blanks of exactly what happened. To her. To us.

Donald Miller once said that good and bad things are happening simultaneously down the roads where each of us lives, connecting us all. Some of us have had our fair share of bad things, haven't we? This is why I chose Laura. It's why she chose me, too. Bad is bad is bad. But then bad turns to gold when we write it down, tell our stories, and watch them transform us or the people we love right before our very eyes.

Laura's stories are my favorite stories. Sometimes, I can barely breathe when I read them. I giggle like a child at her wicked humor. But when she turns the diamond of her writing just enough to refract light into the dark places I've dared not speak of—that haven't yet heard that sacred truth—I let the tears roll down my face without ever sopping them up. Because why would I? They're proof that I'm human; that my friend Laura is a healer.

No one writes Sad-Hopeful like Laura Parrott Perry. Not one other writer.

I hope you are sitting on a couch in whatever home you have, reflecting on the rough places, past or present, and trying like hell to understand what happened. Here is what I believe about the complicated spaces we've survived or found ourselves in. I believe that not all of us have it within us to fully understand them—to grasp the depth of our pain and the deep sense of homelessness we've felt. The ache within our hearts has left so many of us orphaned in one way or another. And this is why we need each other. It's why we need Laura.

In this beautiful memoir, she's already howled at the moon for you, shouldering the massive weight of what it feels like to be alone—this is her gift to us. The work will still be ours to do, but none of what you read here will be so far over your head that you won't be able to catch it and call it to the earth. Because there is gravity in Laura. With both feet on the ground, her life is the road. Her stories, the map forward. And if you've been traveling with a broken compass, Laura has generously left signposts along the way.

She is leading us…homeward.

Last week, I walked the bridges of Cincinnati. Before I set out, I copied and pasted chapter after chapter of *Homeward* into the notes app on my phone. I had already read it but wanted to let it further inside—to see if it might find a homeless corner within me that needed to be spruced up or fully renovated. I wanted to hear my friend's words aloud. So, on my walk, I held down the button on the side of my phone and asked Siri to read them to me, chapter by chapter. Siri read. I listened.

I marveled at Laura's ability to string words together so lovingly. But more than that, I remembered how the people who inspire me the most always balance their pain with forgiveness and mercy, not only for those who've betrayed or let them down, but for themselves as well. How they are able to show me how they got from there, wherever that was, to here.

In each timeworn room Laura enters, you'll watch as she patiently and meticulously surveys the damage. The process of deciding what to take with her and what to leave behind is some of the gentlest sifting I've ever seen. In every bit of grief, I kept hearing her whisper, "thank you." And in every triumph, just the same.

When we are lost, it's so difficult to find our way. But I have this friend, and now you do too, who arranges words and tells stories so therapeutically. And my God, every single time I read them, I see a path forward and heal a little more.

I am still sitting on the same couch. Still in the nicest home I've ever lived in. When I moved here, there were days I'd stand outside and look up at it—nights I'd sit on the roof and watch the city lights flicker across the river. I honestly believed I was finally home. But this big, beautiful house doesn't know a thing about me. Because as Laura's courageous journey has shown me, the search for home is and always will be…inward. Inside our chests. This is where we tear down. This is where we rebuild. This is where we start over.

And so, this is where we must begin.

Chapter One
Exit

"This house is dead. I don't want to be with you anymore."

We have been together for nearly seven years, and friends since we were teenagers.

Twelve words.

My God, that's efficient.

I am sitting on the couch, his. James is sitting in one of the Tiffany blue slipper chairs, mine. He's always loved those chairs because the deep seats are a good fit for his long legs. I used to make him sit down when we argued in college, so I could be taller. College was thirty-one years ago, and I am just so tired. I don't feel like standing.

I look at him across the room. His hazel eyes, my favorite eyes, are averted. He will not look at me. There may as well be an ocean between us. He is solitary—a distant, unreachable shore. He's six feet away, but I can't get to him. To the left of the fireplace, the mantle of which is covered in photos I took and framed for him, is a table. On the table is a yellow sign I bought when he and I first started dating. In grey script it proclaims, *Love Wins.*

Bullshit, I think.

I don't say anything. I don't say one single word. I know if I open my mouth I'll try to convince him this is a mistake, and something, in some deep, primal part of me that I have been refusing to heed for a very long time, won't let me. I know there's nothing to say. I know; I don't understand. I don't understand anything.

I stand and walk up the stairs, slowly. I feel ancient. The boys aren't here. Thank God for that. I walk into the bedroom. His bedroom, I guess. I sit down on the new bed he bought. The bed he bought without me. The one I hate. He threw out my bed.

Shit. I no longer have a bed.

I sit down on his new, awful, stupid bed. It's too tall for me. Perfect for him, which makes sense. It's his bed. My legs dangle over the side like I'm a little girl. I can't seem to feel angry about what's happening, but I am filled with rage that my feet don't touch the ground. I pick my phone up and text my closest friend, Matt.

He just broke up with me. I can't talk right now. I'm okay, but I need you to know.

Then my cousin, Mary. Copy, paste.

Then my friend, Johnny. Copy, paste.

Instinctively, I know I need to tell the truth about this. I know if I don't tell them in real time, I will try very hard not to tell anyone. And if I don't tell anyone, I'll drink. And if I drink, I'll die.

I walk into the closet.

His closet.

I drag a suitcase out. How can it weigh this much when there's nothing in it? I start filling it up. I'm cramming in clothes and shoes and toiletries, and with each empty drawer and every bare hanger, I am leaving this life. His life.

I see my phone lighting up on the nightstand, but I'm too tired to talk to anyone. I can't even bring myself to read their texts. I cannot shoulder anyone else's feelings about this—my own are too heavy. I haven't cried. Can you be too tired to cry? I curl up on the bed and pray for sleep, which eventually comes.

I wake up and for a minute, I forget. The morning sun beaming in through the sliders makes me flinch. We used to sit out on the small porch off the bedroom and listen to music and talk, but that was a long time ago. I look at the pillow next to mine and grief rushes in to fill the empty space.

I walk into the big, beautiful bathroom. His bathroom. I stand in the shower, and slowly turn the temperature fixture all the way. It's searingly hot, but it's the only thing grounding me in the body I keep floating out of. I step onto the white rug and absentmindedly take note of my fiery skin. It looks like it hurts and I suppose it does, but everything's relative. I stand at the vanity I picked out and stare at the exhausted face looking back at me. What shade of lipstick do you wear to leave? Red. Red lipstick is almost always the answer. I wipe the steam off my reflection. I put on makeup, I do my hair.

I have always been great at smoke and mirrors.

I walk out into the bedroom. His bedroom. He is standing there silently, waiting for me. Am I supposed to talk first? I have nothing to say. Finally, he asks me where I am going to go, and I shrug. He asks me to let him know where I end up. Is this concern? Now? I laugh. He makes a move as though to help me with my bags.

I hear myself say, *"No."* The word sounds like it was torn from my throat. I don't recognize my own voice.

I pick up my bags and leave his room. I don't look back. He cannot have that.

I walk past the boys' bedrooms. His boys. I can't think about them yet. I walk back down the staircase which seems to have stretched and grown since the day before. It's a longer walk to leave. James' wretched little Bichon, Bad Dog, trots along beside me. He's a holy terror with most people, but has loved me since the first time I met him. I bend down and scratch him behind the ears. He whines. He wants to be held. Sweet Bad Dog. His dog. I pass by Blu, the dog James acquired while I was away this summer. *Surprise. I made a major life decision without you.* Most definitely his dog. He never pretended otherwise. I think about his bed and his dog and it occurs to me he's been building a new life in front of my eyes—a life that doesn't take me into account, and I just didn't see it. Or wouldn't. If sobriety has taught me nothing else, it's taught me this: I own some of this. I'm a participant.

I can't think about that yet.

I drive down the hill and park my car at the beach. I look out at the tiny sliver of land a half-mile offshore in Long Island Sound. On a summer night, years earlier, we went down for sunset with our next door neighbors. Their son, a sweet and serious little boy, asked me, *"When I grow up, will you move there with me?"* He said he'd be a firefighter and a marine biologist. *"Absolutely,"* I said. He told me the island was called Logo Togo, so its real name ceased to exist and I never called it by any other name, ever again.

For quite some time, I stopped by this beach nearly every day on my ride home to breathe and pray and prepare myself to walk through the front door. From May to October, I circled up here every Sunday morning for a recovery meeting. This rocky little beach has been my Church. The place I've come to rage and laugh and grieve and pray and write. I look at the stretch of sand that has become an integral part of my life. This beach. His beach. I won't be able to walk to it anymore. I can't think about that yet.

It's 80 degrees out, but I'm shivering. The morning sun feels both too bright and not warm enough. It's ridiculous that it's shining. Offensive, even. Mother Nature should really learn how to read the room. A week ago, I'd have been surrounded by cars piled high with chairs and towels and coolers. Children would have been tearing through the sand with their mothers sipping iced coffee and half-heartedly scolding them. Now, the parking lot is empty except for me and an old man sitting next to his station wagon reading the morning paper. The beach doesn't look any different, but there has been a nearly imperceptible shift. Summer is over.

I put on my sunglasses, back my car out, and head to work.

And, just like that, I have no home.

Chapter Two
Harbor

The morning I left James' house, I texted my friend Shabon who was pet-sitting and asked if I could stay with her that night. Our friends were in Bermuda and she was watching their two dogs in their gorgeous house which overlooks a little harbor on the Connecticut shoreline. Shabon said, *"Oh God, Laur. Of course,"* and for the next few days she was a lighthouse; still and bright and guiding.

That first afternoon she brought me coffee, said, *"Here, Beautiful,"* and handed it to me without even looking in my direction. She sat next to me on the porch and stared out at the water in silence. The thing about having friends who have done their work is their ability to sit alongside you in your pain and understand their job description. Shabon very much wanted me to be okay, but she didn't need me to be.

I was in pain, and she let me be.

Grief is not a problem and therefore requires no solution. When you lose a great love it should hurt. We live in a world that tells us pain is to be avoided at all costs, that you should seek to numb or move past it as quickly as possible. The truth is, anything that forestalls you feeling the pain actually prolongs your misery.

I got married at the age of twenty-eight and that marriage lasted fourteen years. When it ended a decade ago, seemingly out of the blue, I did not believe my feelings were survivable. It seemed impossible you could live through that kind of heartbreak, so I ran and numbed and starved and suffered. No amount of wine could keep me out ahead of the crushing grief; no running five times a day on the treadmill and skipping meals could make me disappear fast enough. I did anything and everything to not feel the pain of losing the life I'd built and the marriage I thought would last forever. I signed up for every voluntary pain in order not to feel the loss that felt as though it had been inflicted on me.

I'd spent most of my life awash in shame and keeping secrets. As a survivor of childhood sexual abuse, I'd learned at a very young age that asking for help was futile. Over the years, I adopted coping skills that many survivors turn to in the absence of clinical intervention to help them process trauma. I starved myself to feel some measure of control, and I drank to numb the pain. Those harmful behaviors, which had started off as tools–my best guess at how to survive–had become lethal weapons over time. I had so much unresolved trauma, and so my reaction to my marriage falling to pieces was shame. I didn't take responsibility for the parts that were mine to own, and blamed myself for the things that had nothing to do with me. And because the first lie shame always tells us is that we're alone in what is happening, I told no one. I had no other coping skills, so I hustled and cleaned and volunteered and starved and drank. I hung desperately onto the hope that somehow I could will another person to love me, that I could want the relationship enough for the both of us, and that I could hang onto the home we'd built by my fingernails.

I suppose it may have looked like the pendulum had swung too far in the other direction this time, that I'd over-corrected by seemingly not fighting to work things out once James said it was over, but recovery had taught me to understand surrender. There comes a time in many boxing movies when one of the fighters has lost. Sometimes they know, sometimes they don't–but watching it, we do. The energy of the audience shifts from wanting them to win the fight to wanting them to not die trying. We stop urging them to throw a punch and begin pleading with them to stay down. In the end, surrender is valiant–because there's no losing if you never could have won.

It was over. It was over and I knew it. I didn't want it, but I knew it as surely as I knew anything. And I knew fighting the fact of it would only make things worse. When my marriage ended, I did so much damage because I was unwilling to accept what was happening and let myself feel it. I bought into the notion that if I was heartbroken, I was doing life wrong. But, to love is to risk. Hearts aren't meant to be kept safe. I'd loved with my whole heart and that heart was shattered as a result. Once again, I was standing in the unexpected debris of a life I'd spent years building. The grief and loss were overwhelming and I was determined to feel every minute of it.

The friends whose house I was staying in, Barbara and Leo, would not be home for a couple of days. Shabon was staying in the guest room. The previous year, they'd converted their garage to an in-law suite for Barb's dad. It had French doors that looked out over a tiny harbor, a beautiful little kitchenette and bathroom, a twin bed, and her dad's armchair. It was an airy and serene space, created with great love and intention. Her dad had recently died and I don't think either one of us felt like I should use it, so I slept in their bedroom until they returned. When they got back from their trip, they told me I could stay with them until I found a place, which was unbelievably generous. Unsurprising, because that's just who they are, but still. Barb offered up the in-law apartment. We took to calling it Barb and Leo's Home for Wayward Girls.

Barb and I would sit in her kitchen at night while I tried to process what had happened. Barb is a treasure. She's a social worker–

God bless the social workers. Everyone should have a Barbara. When I'm in the middle of something hard and I need to be sure the other person won't attempt to make me feel better about it by trying to put a cheerful or tidy spin on something painful, she's one of my first calls. She is wise, hilarious, and honest. In a world that loves people to be all one thing, and situations to be black and white, Barb is the sovereign queen of and/both, and Barb sees grey, which is probably what made her such a great therapist. Every now and then she would look at me across the table, shake her head, and say, "*What the FUCK, Lucretia?*" She calls me Lucretia. I'm sure there's a reason, but I can't remember it. That alone made me feel better. Lucretia sounded formidable. Like Maggie Smith would play her in the movie. Lucretia seemed like she might know how to rebuild a life.

For a while, I slept very little. It took me forever to settle down enough to drift off, and I'd wake up most mornings at 2:00 or 3:00 with an increasingly-familiar clutch of anxiety in my chest. I'd try sleep meditations, prayer, melatonin, Netflix–ANYTHING–to quiet my mind and get back to sleep. Nothing worked. I moved through my days in a semi-trance and spent my nights wide awake, staring at the empty spaces in what used to be a full life.

There was a stretch of time during those hard months when I couldn't see the point in going on, when continuing to live seemed exhausting and pointless. I felt like maybe I was just done. I didn't have an active plan, really. It was more of a general mindset that perhaps a terminal diagnosis would be okay. Or an accident. On the longest, darkest nights, maybe something that looked like an accident.

I've always had a perilous tendency to not let people know I was struggling until I was on the other side of it. Somewhere along the line I got the message that the only acceptable pain was in the past. Like, "*I WAS in trouble, but now I'm all healed up and here's what I learned. You're welcome!*" Perspective all wrapped up with a pretty bow. One of my favorite writers, Jen Hatmaker, calls that "tidy testimony." It's a habit I've largely kicked, but when I was in this particular hole it felt different. That is, in part, because my family has been profoundly impacted by suicide and the last thing in the world I wanted was to cause anybody any more pain. There was also part of it that was ego, if I'm being honest. I like to have my shit together. Even now, after all this work, I still hate to ask for help—and let's face it, society tells women we are supposed to make everything look effortless. Even heartbreak.

It's so hard to untangle where grief ends and depression begins. Or maybe sometimes there's no line of demarcation. I have had a couple of years of overwhelming grief. I've lost some relationships so dear to me that even talking about them doesn't feel survivable. I felt disconnected from my family of origin, and then my relationship suddenly ended and I lost my partner and the immediate and extended family that I'd built. I lost the kids I'd helped raise. I lost my home. I lost my neighbors. I lost my pets. And I thought, *"Maybe I can't do this anymore,"* because hand-to-God, what was the actual point? And that didn't feel ominous or scary or crazy.

Sometimes that's what it's like. No dramatic gesture, no active plan. Just this little, seemingly rational voice in the back of your head that constantly tries to negotiate your way out of this world.

I understand suicide in a way I never did before, and I say that as someone who attempted it when I was twelve. I say that as someone who has lost a family member to suicide and had people I love struggle for years with very serious depression. I understand how insidious and pervasive those thoughts can be. I understand how trauma after trauma after loss after loss can build up over the years until you get to a point when it seems pretty logical to consider an exit strategy, because honestly: how much is too much?

The single most powerful thing I have ever heard at a recovery meeting came out of the mouth of an angel-faced teenage girl. She said, *"My disease speaks to me in my own voice."* I just about flipped the table when she said it. I have never heard a truer thing in my life.

The voice suggesting I might be done wasn't frightening. The opposite, actually. It was reassuring. It felt like a compassionate voice, a calm voice offering a perspective worth considering. The voice telling me it might be time to go didn't feel like a problem; it felt like a solution. That's the thing about depression, it's a dark and slippery cliff and the closer you are to the edge, the less able you are to watch your step.

At night, I'd lie alone in the twin bed in the beautiful little apartment and wonder if there was a way to leave that wouldn't hurt anyone else.

I had two incredible people upstairs, one, a trained therapist, whom I could have turned to for help. I had a deep, wide, wonderful recovery community who loved me and would have done absolutely *anything* to make sure I was okay. I had good friends who were a phone call away. I had co-workers who cared deeply about me and were trained in mental health and addiction. I had health insurance and lots of knowledge and connections.

I was about as resourced as a woman could be—but none of that mattered at 3:00 a.m., because despair doesn't care who you know.

I once heard the author Rob Bell define despair as the belief that tomorrow will be exactly like today. That makes so much sense to me. And when today is unbearable? Leaving seems sensible.

People marveled at my strength, how well I was handling things, and how resilient I was. But I was not doing well, and while I do believe I am resilient, I think it's a mistake to believe we never lose strong, resilient people to depression.

I had times when the veneer would slip. One of my co-workers, Shelley, could see past it. She is brilliant and funny and fierce, and she and I are wired pretty similarly. I don't respond to touchy-feely, sentimental, "there-there" stuff. At all. It actually makes me feel angry and lonely when people come at me like that. That is not how Shelley rolls. She came into my office one day in the middle of all the things, sat down in the chair next to my desk, looked me straight in the eye and said, pointedly, in her Southern twang that always seems funny in contrast to her no-bullshit, direct manner, *"Hey. You okay?"* I immediately started to cry. I told her about the circumstances, not where those circumstances had taken me. I told her about the losses. I didn't tell her about the hole I was in. When I was done talking, she looked at me intently, nodded once and said, *"What do you need?"*

I had no earthly idea how to answer that question. I'm sure I said, *"Nothing."* And I'm sure I was furious at myself for crying. I always am. I'm equally sure I fixed my makeup, finished smiling my way through the work day, crawled into bed that night and thought about dying. I had so many people who knew what was going on and were concerned about me–they knew the facts, anyway–but even given all the work I'd done, my go-to coping skills still provided cover for the dark place I was in. I smiled at people, put on a cute outfit every day, and didn't miss a day of work. I wasn't trying to fool other people into thinking I was okay as much as I was hoping that if I continued to act as though I didn't want to die it might lead to actually feeling that way. The very things I was doing to survive being in the hole masked the fact I was in one.

I think about it all the time–the number of people we encounter every day who are fighting life-threatening things we know nothing about. Depression, addiction, trauma, grief… they so often don't look the way we expect them to. We lose people to battles we don't even know they're in. Cause of death: Fine on the outside.

It's like that first scene in the movie *Jaws* where the young woman runs naked down to the water. It's a beautiful summer night and she's swimming and laughing. It's quiet, and the water is placid. Then there's a sudden violent tug downward. She screams, but it doesn't matter, because no one on the shore can hear her. And then she's gone. Barely a ripple.

My ex-husband once showed me a video of a man paddleboarding off the coast of California. He was wearing a Go-Pro and swimming around underneath his board was an enormous great white shark. It was completely silent. I said that the most terrifying thing about it was the lack of sound. My ex laughed at me and asked if I thought there should be music. *"YES!"* I said. John Williams created the perfect two-note alarm for our manufactured terror but in real life, sometimes imminent danger is quiet and stalks us, undetected.

I know what I would have said to someone else who was in the deep, dark hole I was in because I have said it. I have counseled people, advised people, and resourced people who were on the edge. I've taken them to meetings and driven them to rehab. I've held friends' hands in the night, visited them in psych wards, and recommended therapy, and a hundred other things.

I know it all, and none of that knowledge made a damned bit of difference during those brutal months, because the chasm between head and heart when it comes to these things is a million miles wide, and countless fathoms deep.

Every morning during that awful time, I went to a 7:00 a.m. recovery meeting. I had been sober for nearly five years at that point, and I'd learned enough to know that the fact I didn't want to go was a clear indicator that I needed to. I may not have told the whole truth about where I was at, but each morning I circled up with alcoholics, let them love me, and didn't drink, no matter what. There are few things in life I know for sure, but I can tell you with one hundred percent certainty that if I had picked up a drink during that time, I would not be here to tell this story.

Every day felt like I was trying to walk through jello. It took enormous effort to do everything, including nothing. I found myself saying *"Okay,"* a lot. Like, I'd get in the car, take a deep breath, and say, *"Okay,"* and then go to work. When people insisted I eat and put food in front of me, *"Okay."* Over and over: *"What's next?"* And then, *"Okay."* But no matter how many times I said it, I was not okay.

In her book, *The Long Night: Readings and Stories to Help You through Depression*, my friend Jessica Kantrowitz writes; *"You are not alone and this will not last forever."* It's such a beautifully reassuring mantra, and it is true. It just doesn't *feel* true when you're in the middle of it, which is why her constant benediction on social media is so incredibly important. The thing about being in that hole is that you lose all perspective, and you forget that the discernible difference between being hopelessly lost and nearly found is *nothing*–they feel exactly the same.

Eventually, the light began to come back. The initial shock wore off and things started to come together. I found a place to live and made plans. I began to dismantle what was no longer my home. I made use of James's absence on business trips to empty out my side of his closet and clean out what used to be my office. I began to sleep a little easier–at least I fell asleep easier. I started to eat unprompted again; I even laughed again, which felt like a miracle. It started to seem as though tomorrow could be different–maybe not better, but not the same–and that the sun rising was not a thing to be dreaded.

Still, most mornings I woke up in the predawn hours with that feeling, like a steamer trunk on my chest. I'd get up and peek out at the little body of water across the street. Autumn was here, so it was chilly and dark, and all the boats were moored and protected. You can do that when the storms are predictable and you know about a harsh season in advance. Having grown up in New England, I'm always bemused by people scrambling to cope with the first snowfall each year. I've been known to snarkily say that winter is never a surprise. I guess it's true we know that winter follows autumn, but even given that inevitability, we can still find ourselves wholly unprepared for the sudden brutality of the change of seasons. Perhaps I should not have been blindsided by the upending of my life, but I was.

In the nights leading up to the move, I lay in bed thinking about how much had changed. I was moving into a new place. I would be leaving the town where I got sober, so I would need to build a new recovery community. For the first time in my adult life,

I wasn't responsible for anyone but me. And I'd be living in a city for the first time, which could only mean at some point I would have to parallel park.

They were terrifying times.

I was no longer in my old home, not yet in my new one. I didn't have my things. I felt like a guest in my own life. I found myself perched on the fault line between a life that no longer existed and the one I would need to create. The earthquake was over, but the tectonic plates had rearranged themselves in such a way that the landscape was unfamiliar. Even the horizon wasn't where I left it.

I've never done well with uncertainty. Before I got sober, I could handle catastrophe better than I could handle not knowing what was going to happen. Come the zombie apocalypse, I'm your girl. I'll have water, batteries, and a plan. The period when we're wondering if there'll *be* a zombie apocalypse? Forget about it. I'm on the floor. I have friends who call this being "in the hallway." Even that analogy freaked me out. I just wanted to pick a damned door, hang a freaking wreath on it, and go inside.

When I packed up my office at James' house, I found a smooth rock engraved with the words, *Begin Again.* A friend had given it to me when I was going through my divorce. It was right there on my desk, but it had become invisible over time, the way things do when you don't need them. Looking at it, the words didn't feel inspirational. They felt aggressive. I felt defeated as I ran my fingers over the recessed letters. *Begin Again.* It was exhausting to even think about. I was forty-eight years old and it felt ludicrous to have to start over. I hovered in this space between petulance and despair. I wanted to stomp my feet, or else die. I thought, *I don't want to start over. I don't want to decide where the towels go again. I can't possibly make decisions about cabinets and parking and utilities.*

I don't want to.

I don't want to.

I don't want to.

I didn't want *any* of it. I slipped the rock in my purse anyway, and used it like a worry-stone.

When it was time to leave Barb and Leo's house, I was terrified. I didn't know what it would be like to come home and have no one to talk to. No one to feed. No kids to clean up after. No dog to walk. No partner to ask how my day was. No one who needed me. No one who really knew me. Strangers are so easy to fool. All you do is distract them with a smile and chirp, "*I'm fine!!!!!*" and they never see the fin circling.

The onset of the demise of my marriage had come out of the blue as well. Or at least, that's how it felt at the time. I was astonished by the news that my marriage was not what I'd thought it to be, and rather than anger at the news, I felt shame and told no one. I went to PTA meetings, smiled, wore cute clothes, and had the right countertops, so I was obviously fine. Except, I was spiraling into alcoholism and starving myself. I was drinking every night, my hair was falling out, my gums were bleeding, and my clothes were falling off my body. During that time, I got positive affirmations for how I looked *every single day*. My disappearing act had a cheering section.

I know so many people who espouse 'fake it til you make it,' but I have a healthy fear of my preternatural ability to appear fine when I'm actively dying. I've come to understand that faking it has a body count attached to it. I'd been taught to show up jacked-up in recovery, and my community knew me well enough to raise their collective eyebrow at my attempts at 'fine-ness,' which was part of why I was so worried about moving away. How do you walk the line of being honest and clear about the fact that you are in trouble but also function in the world and meet your responsibilities? It's the tightest of tightropes and even harder to pull off when you're not surrounded by people who know your history and your tells.

The last morning at The Home for Wayward Girls, I looked out the French doors at the sunrise glinting off the water. I sat in Barb's dad's recliner, where I'd curled up every night, shivering, wrapped in blankets, trying desperately to understand why my life had been blown apart again. What had been my part in it? And how had I let myself fall for the idea of home again? Because that's what it felt like: I felt stupid. Like I'd been duped. Like I fell for the idea of safety and belonging *again*. Like I'd learned *nothing*.

One day, early in my stay, I'd come back from work and Barb was emptying out the closet for me. Her father's clothes lay in neat stacks on the bed. She lifted one of his shirts to her face and breathed in deeply. My eyes stung, because I was still wearing James' white button-down dress shirt to bed every night. I hadn't washed it. It didn't even smell like him anymore, because I'd co-opted it so long ago. But it smelled like his closet. It smelled like his laundry detergent. It smelled like home, and watching Barb inhale the memory of her dad brought an ache to my throat. I completely understood the attachment to the pedestrian souvenirs of a lost love. I demurred, saying I didn't need the closet and that I understood emptying it would probably be too painful for her. She talked about how much it had meant to her to create this space for her dad, who she adored, and that it made her happy to think of me using the space to heal.

Truth be told, I was afraid to hang my things in that closet. Afraid to settle in. Afraid to exhale. I was afraid of everything. Every single thing. But Barb is loving and bossy, and she won. I hung my clothes, only to pack them up in a couple of months to move to a new apartment in New Haven, Connecticut. Moving forward and looking back.

Chapter Three
Tide

The summer before James ended things, I began stopping by the beach at the bottom of the hill from our house nearly every evening on my drive home from work. It was usually just this side of sunset, so the harsh summer sun had softened enough that umbrellas were being folded and the few little kids who were still playing at the water's edge did so with a renewed energy fueled by the slight drop in temperature. It was an in-between time along the shore. The majority of the day-trippers had gone home to rinse off the salt and sand and sit down to eat, but the influx of teenagers smuggling booze onto the beach in water bottles was still a few hours away.

I needed to get home, but I felt like I had to brace myself, because maybe things would be okay when I walked through the front door and maybe they wouldn't. It wasn't that things were universally terrible or hard; in some ways that would have been easier. I just didn't ever know—and in times of uncertainty, the ocean is nearly always the answer, regardless of the question.

What that usually looked like was me sitting by the water's edge talking to Matt or Mary or Judy or Johnny. They didn't know I was parked down the street from my house trying to summon up the courage to walk through my own front door, and they didn't need to. They were my safe places, and talking to them centered me. If I couldn't reach one of them, or the truth was too near the tip of my tongue, I'd turn the volume up and let Brandi Carlile, or Shawn Colvin, or The Chicks or Alanis loan me some of their bravery.

Britannica.com defines pattern as, *"the regular and repeated way in which something happens or is done."* Looking back, I can see my pattern of being unwilling to address circumstances in my relationships that were no longer healthy or working. The pattern was me, prioritizing the illusion of safety over honesty. The pattern was me being willing to stay in a life which required me to steel myself to walk into it each night, and also unwilling to examine why this nightly pit stop had become a necessity.

The beach had always been a place that helped me remember the scale of things. I could peer out at the horizon, which very much looked like the end of the world, and know that it wasn't. It felt hopeful, somehow, to know there is so much that was beyond what I could perceive from my vantage point. Confronted by the vast sea under the endless sky, I remembered how small I was -- because the ocean doesn't care.

I don't know why I find that comforting, but I do.

Every summer, the town we lived in hauled in trucks full of sand and tried to make our rocky little New England beach a softer, gentler place, and every year Mother Nature laughed. Every year, the tide would come in and drag out to sea the expensive, generic sand trucked in by men who would try to exert their will over things far above their pay grade. When will we learn we can't make things what they're not? And by we, I mean I.

Sunday mornings, from spring until autumn, I circled up on that beach for a recovery meeting with my band of troublemakers. We came to that little stretch of shore on the Long Island Sound to tell the truth and ask for help. The summer I stopped drinking, I'd sit on the outskirts of the group, drinking my coffee and trying to decide if sobriety was a thing I could do. I'd listen to people share, and I'd watch the gulls brazenly walk through our circle, pecking in the sand while we fought for our lives.

I guess we were all just looking for our daily bread.

Over time, I moved in closer. I learned to listen. I made friends. Some stayed. Some left. Some died. People leave and people die, and we'd find ourselves with gaps in the circle. For a while, the gaps would be all we could see, but over time I learned the gaps do not remain. We'd close ranks to grieve. The circle would shrink in fear, which hovered over us like a shadow—a palpable presence that seemed tangible, but wasn't. Then, someone would raise their hand and say they were new. They'd ask for help and we'd widen the circle again.

We'd make more room because the circle breathes. It expands and contracts and expands again. People come, we welcome. They go, we worry. They come back, we celebrate. They die, we grieve. But then I'd see that shimmer of grace, which always seems ephemeral but is as real and solid as the rocks in the jetty that arcs out from the beach where we gather.

Most nights I'd pull into the parking lot at the beach and phone a friend, watch the gulls, or listen to music. I'd remember that the world is big and I am small and that everything, everything, everything is temporary. It helped me to breathe. I was so sure the difficult time would pass and that we would come out the other side of it. I was certain of it. It was hard, but love doesn't quit, right? I'd park for ten minutes or so, looking out over the water at the trees of Logo Togo on the horizon.

When the tide is really low, a sand bar appears like a bridge to the island and you can walk to it. It looks easy to reach, but you need to be careful because when the tide turns you have limited time to get out before you're in real trouble, and the ocean doesn't care about your plans.

James and I always talked about going.

The tide comes in, and the tide goes out, and the ocean doesn't care. Galileo theorized the movement of the waves was proof that the earth moved. His hypothesis about tides was incorrect, but his larger theory, that the earth was not the center of the universe, was sound. The ocean didn't care that things were hard, and in some ways, that very indifference is what made the beach a safe place for me. Because this beach was where I came each weekend to be reminded that I am not the center of the universe, either.

I'd sit and wait until the sound of my friends' voices, the music, or the waves brought me back to center, and I was ready to drive up the hill to the house I called home.

Chapter Four
Haven

The late afternoon sun streamed in through the four huge windows of the apartment, casting golden light on the oak floors patched over decades with planks of varying widths. I loved how imperfect they were. The vaulted ceilings were tall and airy with exposed beams, pipes, and ductwork. The corridor leading to the elevator sloped downward and there were sudden level changes–steps where you wouldn't expect them. It was disorienting at times because everything was a little off-kilter, which felt right because so was I.

Down in the courtyard, there was a gazebo and a path lined with old-fashioned looking lamps. A giant, dormant smokestack loomed over the quiet little oasis in the middle of the city. There were racks of bikes along the weathered and patched brick wall leading out to an archway with a wrought iron gate which opened out to the city sidewalk. The whole place seemed like it had stories to tell.

The building was a converted factory–home to the first corset manufacturer in the United States, and the exclusive maker of "Dr. Scott's Electric Corsets," which apparently promised to cure nervousness and a host of other ailments thought to be peculiar to the female sex. I would lie in bed at night with the windows open listening to the trains go through the nearby station, imagining a building full of workers fashioning tight, zappy cages for anxious women to walk around in.

I've heard people say that train horns are quite a melancholy sound, but as lonely as I was, they didn't strike me that way. There was something reassuring about them. They sounded like an invitation or a promise. Out there in the night, passengers were on their way somewhere, maybe headed someplace exciting and new. I didn't feel that way. This unwelcome new path I was on felt like an adventure in the same way being a member of the Donner party was an adventure. Maybe it met the criteria for unexpected and dramatic, but it was slightly lacking on the fun front. Even so, it helped to remember that life goes on, sometimes with unforgivable determination, and that somewhere out there in the dark city night, people were living theirs.

I went to some new recovery meetings but none of them felt comfortable. Who were these new alcoholics? I wanted my familiar cozy church basement filled with people I knew and loved. The thought of making new friends felt like a lot of work, and my old friends had full lives. The thing about a sudden loss is that people rush in to support you, but eventually regular life resumes, even when you don't have one.

Thanksgiving was looming. Thanksgiving is a holiday with so much built-in nostalgia as to render it unbearable for people who find themselves in seasons of loss. The day, centered on gathering and tradition and gratitude, seemed only to amplify loneliness and highlight empty chairs.

My cousin Mary wanted me to come to Massachusetts, but that felt impossible. I had several friends invite me to their dinners, but the thought of being an outlier to someone else's family gathering felt lonelier than being alone. My friend Laurie, who lived down the hall in my new building, always held an 'Orphans' Thanksgiving' for people who didn't have a place to go. I went for a bit, but left early to sit alone in my apartment. I'd cooked a parallel meal, because I couldn't imagine not cooking, but then I sat there looking at my sad little turkey and all the trimmings, none of which I wanted to eat.

My apartment was hot from having the oven on all day, so I went for a walk in the park a block from my building. I shivered as the chilly night air crept through my jacket and underneath the red scarf twined around my neck. The park was ringed with brownstones and townhouses, and a huge church anchored one side. The final, angled rays of the setting sun turned the steeple a deep coral. As the streetlamps came on, I walked, kicking at the piles of leaves on the zig-zag paths. In the burgeoning darkness the windows were illuminated, and here and there I could see rooms full of people either eating or cleaning up. I didn't want to go home to my empty apartment, but I didn't want to make a spectator sport of this day of togetherness, either. I didn't want to go back to my friend's place, though I could have.

I didn't want to be anywhere I could be.

I'd been fighting tears all day, trying to make the best of things, but as the overwhelming sadness rose up in me, I stood still in the center of the park and let them come. I wondered if James and the boys had gone to New York to be with his family. I was sure they had. I pictured the lunacy that always ensued with a gaggle of cousins tearing around the house, laughing hysterically, driving each other and the adults crazy, with multiple dogs underfoot, and too many cooks in the kitchen. There were times during those holidays when I would need to step outside for some calm and solitude, but standing alone in the park, in the strangely quiet city night, all I wanted was to be overwhelmed and exasperated in the middle of all of that familiar chaos.

Chapter Five
Rescue

I'd only been in my apartment a few weeks when loneliness eventually led me to porn. And, by porn, obviously, I mean Petfinder.

Every night I would try to watch TV, but I couldn't follow plots. It seemed as though everything was Christmas-related and the holidays were a big, steaming pile of nope for me. Everything was stupid or sad or happy or medium. All of it was untenable. None of it could be tenned.

I kept trying to read and couldn't, which had only ever happened one other time in my life. The year after my marriage blew up I lost the ability to read anything other than labels. Primarily wine labels, but whatever. I couldn't focus, I couldn't retain information. I took no joy in stories. When I got sober and reflected on that time, I came to understand I was deeply depressed—and self-medicating with a depressant, which, as it turns out, is not terribly effective. The crushing headaches that accompanied every morning would only be alleviated by the evening, and by that point I'd be drinking again. Reading had always been my solace when I wanted to escape, and at a time when I most wanted to be in any story but my own, I'd lost the option of losing myself in the pages of somebody else's.

I worked on the assumption that given the fact I spent most evenings lying in bed thinking about how nice it would be to not wake up, I was probably depressed again. Stillness and quiet were unbearable. I didn't want to *be*, I wanted to *do*. I was fine at work. People needed me there. I was busy, and there were a million things to be done. But then, I'd get home to the achingly empty apartment and I had no idea how to do life. No point in cooking, because I had no appetite. Drinking myself into oblivion was no longer an option. No TV. No books. No social life because I hadn't been single in so long I didn't even know what that looked like. I hadn't really been alone since I was 21, the year I had my first child. I was singularly unprepared for motherhood, but my son became my sun. My reason for everything. I became an instant family when he was born and had been a part of a family system ever since.

I had no partner, no kids at home. No pets. Just a couple of plants my cousin Mary made me buy. And as I'd been given strict instructions on how not to love them to death, they only needed me for about 45 seconds once a week.

I needed another sentient being. Preferably, a four-legged one.

My perfect dog had died two years earlier, and I lost James' dogs in the break up. Trolling for puppies was about the only thing I could handle. It was the first time in 28 years I was not responsible for another living creature and I felt adrift.

I came across a little doggo named Fred. He was white and looked pretty dumb, which may not be a laudable quality in a human friend but is actually a fairly solid character trait in a dog. The write-up said he had a great personality and loved life. I started to stalk Fred. Why wasn't anyone adopting him? He was so cute! And his name was Fred! I started to flirt with the idea of adopting him. I planned to change his name to Kevin for no good reason whatsoever.

Eventually, I was ready to stop window shopping, so I made the call to go meet Fred. Just meet him. Like a coffee date. Not *dinner* or anything. No big commitment. I reached out and made an appointment. He was being fostered through a rescue organization in the next town. When I pulled up, I met Mike, the man who ran the place. He and I had been texting back and forth to arrange the meet and greet. In our exchange, he asked me if I wanted to meet any other dogs while I was there.

I'd written a whole love story for Fred/Kevin and me, but the guy was so earnest I felt like I should do my due diligence. Plus, dogs are good. More dogs = more good. When I arrived, Mike led me into the house where there were multiple crates. He brought out one dog named Ginger. She was the color of a new penny and very sweet, but neither of us was super drawn to each other. Then he said, *"I think you might like Susie."*

He unlatched the crate door, and a skinny white dog with black spots, including a blaze over one eye and a giant polka dot on her butt right above her tail, came out. She was hesitant, and her ears went down and back, initially. She looked afraid. We made eye contact, and, as soon as we did, her ears stood at attention and she ran over and jumped up on me. I laughed and started scratching those expressive ears, which were spotted and velvety. She looked straight at me with her beautiful golden brown eyes which were fringed in long white lashes. Then she leaned against me and put her head on my shoulder.

Uh-oh, I thought. *Settle down, Susie. I'm here for Fred/Kevin.*

Susie and I cuddled for a bit. She was a funny mix of timid and rambunctious. She was clearly smart and supermodel gorgeous. She was the Linda Evangelista of rescue dogs.

Then it was time to meet Fred/Kevin. Mike said that he was "out back" in a special "shed." *Huh*, I thought. As we approached the Special Area, Mike suggested I stand back, and mentioned that Fred was "energetic."

When he opened the door, a smallish white blur shot past me into the enclosed area. I didn't think those color trails you see in cartoons were a real thing, but in true Roadrunner fashion, Fred/Kevin hurtled around the Special Area with a white comet tail behind him. The small, muscular, white entity careened around the pen, seemingly propelled by what I can only assume were booster rockets.

Apparently, a team of neuroscientists from MIT found that the human brain can process entire images that the eye sees for as little as 13 milliseconds. I am sure that they are right, but hand-to-God I'd not be able to pick Fred/Kevin out of a dog line-up because he wouldn't stay still long enough for my eyeballs to relay any information to my brain. Mike looked at me out of the corner of his eye and chuckled. *"The thing about Fred is, he might not be an 'apartment' dog."* I tried to imagine what I would come home to if he was left alone while I was at work. The term "Shock and Awe" came to mind. *"I just feel like... Fred maybe needs a... a farm of some sort? With...acreage?"* Mike laughed again.

It didn't feel great to walk away, but it didn't feel as bad as coming home to a Fred/Kevin shaped hole in the wall of my apartment because he'd made a Kool-Aid-Man style break for it during the day, which was the most optimistic outcome I could imagine. I said a prayer for his adoption by an energetic farmer/scientist who might be able to find a way to harness Fred's specialness into some sort of renewable energy source that would save the world.

I walked back to the house making a mental note that "personality" on a dog adoption website is akin to "charm" on a real estate website. Trouble.

I asked to see Susie again and Mike smiled. I considered gently reminding him that no one likes a know-it-all. I played with her for a few minutes and told him I wanted to think about it. I got all the way to the first red light on my way home before I texted him and told him I was a goner. He texted back, *"I had a feeling about you two."* Whatever, Mike.

I sat on the couch that night looking at Susie's profile on Petfinder. That was as close as I planned to get to dating apps. She was so gorgeous, but *Susie* was not going to cut it. And she certainly wasn't a Kevin.

I looked over my laptop screen at the stack of books I'd piled on the ottoman in an attempt to get myself reading again. I'd pulled down a few of my favorites with the thought that perhaps something I'd read many times would be a good re-entry. *A Prayer for Owen Meany, Bird by Bird, Pride and Prejudice*, and various Brene Brown books lay there, unread. On the top of the pile was my dog-eared copy of *To Kill A Mockingbird*. I remembered the first time I read it, and how I fell in love with the brave, tenderhearted, inquisitive daughter of Atticus Finch. I smiled as I pictured the curious, sensitive, fierce little creature I was about to bring into my life.

"*Scout*," I said out loud. She was Scout.

I went to pick Scout up on a rainy December night. She was being fostered by a sweet couple who lived in a town just outside New Haven. When I arrived, they welcomed me into their home and it very quickly became apparent they were more than a little in love with the dog they were about to hand off to me. Multiple times, they mentioned that if they were not about to move to Hawaii to live with their son, they would be adopting her themselves. I thanked them profusely for taking such good care of her and got their phone numbers so I could text them photos of her in her new home. They gave me a bag of her food, a toy she loved, and said their goodbyes.

We walked down the long, wet driveway to my car, parked in the halo of a streetlight. Scout's ears were down and it was hard to know whether she was nervous heading off with a stranger, or if this Texas-born girl was just not down with the cold, New England winter night. I opened the car door and helped scootch her into the front seat. She immediately got down on the floor and stayed there, peeking up at me.

I talked to her the whole ride home. A few minutes in, she hopped back up on the seat and curled up, putting her snout on the center console. I reached over and started petting her while I drove. She pulled her head back, unsure, and then sniffed my hand. I thought about how strange her life had been. She was a stray on the streets of Houston, then at the pound just days away from being euthanized. She was saved by a woman who was there to adopt another dog and when she heard Scout's days were numbered, she brought her home as well and contacted a rescue organization that transports dogs from the South up North to be adopted.

She'd probably just gotten used to her foster family, and here I was bringing her to another new place. She had no way of knowing that she was going home, because she had no way of knowing what that might even mean.

We pulled into my building's lot, walked into the lobby, and got on the elevator. Another tenant got on at the same time and said, *"Oh, cute dog! Is she friendly?"* Hell if I know, I thought. *"I just adopted her, so we're still getting to know each other,"* I said. He smiled. *"Aw, that's sweet! Her forever home!"* Sure, I thought. Assuming there is such a thing.

The elevator doors shut and we began the ascent. Scout hit the deck. I crouched down next to her and rubbed her soft ears. *"It's okay, girl. You're okay."* I knew that she didn't believe that yet, and why should she? She was with a total stranger, she was freaked out in this new and scary place, and she had no earthly idea what her future held. We had so much in common already!

We walked into the apartment and I fed her right away. I put some of her new toys out and positioned her bed just so. She walked around, sniffing in all the corners. Every noise startled her. I sat and watched her. After she'd done some exploring, she came over to where I was sitting and hopped up on the couch. I scratched her nose and gave her a kiss on the blaze over her left eye. *"We'll figure it out, Scout. I promise."*

That first night we both slept on the couch, curled up at opposite ends. Alone, together.

Chapter Six
Shelter

When I started looking for a new place to live, I instinctively knew I needed to be around people. Excluding college, it would be the first time in my life I'd not lived in the suburbs. When looking for my new place, I'd not had to consider school districts or yard size, because it was just me. New Haven was only twenty minutes away, but it was a completely different life. When I moved, I had a vision of becoming part of the fabric of the community, eating at restaurants, going to the theater, making new friends, and building a new recovery network. I was going to make the city my home.

And then, just a few months in, the pandemic hit.

All of a sudden, I was expected to stay inside the place that didn't yet feel like home. Restaurants were only open for delivery or curbside pickup, theaters closed down overnight. Groceries were being delivered, or else you went to the supermarket and stood, socially distanced, in lines being counted as you went into stores that had become obstacle courses with arrows and lines indicating you should STAND BACK.

My job had gone completely virtual, so there was no separation between work and life, nothing was open, and everyone was staying inside. You might think that would make it easier to feel like it was really my home, but the opposite was true. It felt a little like early sobriety to me–the jangly nerves, the intense emotions welling up all the time, and the sense that I was being asked to do the impossible.

Prior to the shutdown, I knew the city as a bustling place; loud, with people rushing everywhere. My new apartment was right near downtown, so the streets were full of shoppers, workers, and traffic. It's so easy not to see people when it's like that. In all that noise and with that much busy-ness, anonymity–hell, invisibility–is easier.

I found myself wondering about the people seeking shelter in the unlit store entryways. How did they get to a place where they had no home? What series of events and circumstances led to that? Poverty? Addiction? Mental illness? Trauma? Bad luck? All of the above? I'd found myself without a home suddenly, but I had layers of privilege, family, and community. I was sober and employed. I had health insurance. I had a certain amount of built-in protection, which might feel like immunity, but the reality is that the cracks vulnerable people fall through get bigger all the time.

When I first got her, Scout was not a fan of the chaos downtown, so I got in the routine of walking her before dawn to try and ease her into city life. Her stop-drop-and-roll routine every time a garbage truck rumbled by was less of an issue when we were the only ones out and about. Roaming the streets so early in the morning, I was introduced to a different city than the one I knew before. When it's that quiet, people's stories are louder.

I made it a point to linger by the bus stops while the buses were idling so she could start to acclimate to the sights and sounds in her new environment. I was standing there one particularly cold morning, and I was startled by a voice behind me. I peered into the shadowy doorway. It was an older gentleman who had spoken to me the previous day when I walked by with her; he'd commented that she was a beauty. He was wrapped in a faded red blanket and leaning up against a sizable, worn duffel bag. When I recognized him, I said hello and said something about trying to get her used to the noise in the hope she'd stop being so frightened by it.

He said, "*The city sure can be a scary place. She's smart, though. She'll be okay.*" "*Your mouth to God's ears,*" I replied. "*Indeed,*" he laughed wheezily. "*Indeed.*" He asked me what her name was, and I told him. "*Scout. That's a good name. That's a brave name.*" I smiled, looked down at my skittish little dog, and agreed. In my experience, more often than not, brave and terrified go hand in hand.

As the weeks unfolded and COVID-19 wreaked havoc on the world, the energy of the city shifted. The streets were pretty much empty all day long, and we could walk without having to navigate around other people. There were no more delivery trucks to petrify her because there were no more deliveries.

Most of the shelters initially closed their doors, so when I walked through the city square, I began to see even more people sleeping on benches, in alleys, and in the doorways of shops that wouldn't be opening come daybreak. It felt like the first time I walked Scout in the park after a snowfall. There was seemingly a 1000% increase in the number of squirrels overnight, but really the squirrels had always been there—they were just suddenly visible because the rest of the background had faded to white. In the absence of shelters to sleep in, coffee shops and libraries for people to use restrooms and get warm in, and the distracting hustle and bustle of daily city life, the homeless–our underserved sisters and brothers–were suddenly front and center. In the end, maybe it's less that they stopped being invisible and more that we stopped being so blind.

Walking through my favorite stretch of shops just outside the Yale campus, I glanced at windows that were papered over, and grates that remained down over the doors all day. It felt like a war zone. Initially, business owners put signs up saying they'd be re-opening soon–signs whose edges would eventually curl, as week after week went by, only to be replaced by signs expressing gratitude to their customers and sorrow that they were closing permanently.

I was getting to know a version of the city that hadn't existed a few weeks ago. A city full of people yearning to get out of their homes and people dying to get into one. We were a city that had lost its sense of urgency. It was a city with nowhere to be and nothing to do. A city without a pulse.

I sat on my chocolate brown velvet couch watching the sunset turn the tall sloped walls crimson. The glass candlesticks on my new dining room table glowed pink. My art had been hung, my clothes were in the closet. The cabinets were crammed full of my cookware that used to reside in a larger kitchen, and perhaps most importantly, the bookcases were full of my books. I was surrounded by my things again–things I had accumulated over the nearly fifty years I had been alive.

It was all familiar. *Ish.* Like when you see someone you know, but they're out of context, so you can't quite place them. I remember one time being at the grocery store with my youngest and they saw their first grade teacher in the produce aisle. They recognized her but had a hard time accepting it was actually *her.* In the wild. They were all but unable to speak at the unsettling experience of seeing her shop like a regular human. *You mean to say she EATS?*

Just wait till all these pandemic kiddos find out their teachers have legs. Minds will be blown.

As I sat there in the waning light, my very favorite time of day, surrounded by my beautiful, familiar things, it was just like seeing Mrs. Spong buying broccoli all over again. I accepted that I lived there, but I could not fucking believe I lived there.

I was homesick as hell, in the place where I lived.

In the early days, they told us it might be up to six weeks of sheltering in place. *Six whole weeks.* Bless our unsuspecting hearts. Every time someone mentioned that seemingly impossible length of time being isolated, I laughed the high-pitched cackle that's a tell to anyone who knows me that I am not okay. I said to friends over and over again, *'I am not going to be able to do this.'* In short order, there were billboards everywhere exhorting me to STAY HOME when I'd just landed in a new place in a new city and I didn't even know what that meant. It was a beautiful apartment, but it was not home. I was still in the stages of waking up a little disoriented and having to mentally acclimate.

Wait. Where am I? Oh right. It's over. He stopped loving me. On a dime. Kids, house, dogs, neighborhood–the life I'd help build for almost seven years was yanked out from under me like a tablecloth at some shitty, two-bit magic show. Gone.

Most mornings, post eye-opening, pre-coffee, involved a surge of grief.

I would open my eyes, adjust to my surroundings, remember, and then… slam.

A couple of years ago, I was with James at the beach on Cape Cod. We were standing in the water and the waves were intense. He was laughing at my stubbornness. I kept bracing myself for the waves, and when they came, no matter what I did, I'd get knocked flat. Then I'd get up, and do it again. Like somehow I could prepare for and withstand the sea. Like I could dig in enough to win against what the moon set into motion.

There are those times when you can see grief coming and try to prepare for it, but I honestly think grief is more often like a tsunami. When I was younger, I always envisioned tsunamis to be massively tall tidal waves that towered over everything on land. Now I know that, more often than not, it's not the height of the wave that does the destroying. It's the unanticipated, unthinkably powerful surge. Not some enormous wall of water you can see coming a mile off–if it were, you might be able to escape. No, it's just a ruinous force of nature brought about by some distant event that sneaks up, takes you out at the knees, and lays waste to everything in its path.

Maybe when we say we are homesick what we are actually feeling is grief. Grief for a time or place or reality that we no longer have access to, or never did. The Welsh actually have a poetic word for it, because of course they do. *Hiraeth*. There's no exact translation, but Collins English Dictionary defines *hiraeth* as, "a nostalgic longing for a place which can never be revisited." Was I grieving the home I lost in the break-up, or was I grieving something deeper?

My homesickness was more complicated than the death of my relationship and all that went along with it. It touched on old, deep, unhealed wounds. There was plenty to mourn in the losses I'd just sustained, but the deep, wide river of grief I found myself in had the watershed moments of my childhood as its source. I don't ever remember not having that ache, that hunger, that yearning. The reality is, I have been homesick my whole damned life. Homesick for safety and belonging, connection and truth. For me, the idea of home has always been just out of reach.

Chapter Seven
Sundays

Spring lasted an eternity in the first year of the pandemic. We'd been in that liminal space for what seemed like a long time: no longer the raw days of a painful winter, not yet the warm days of a beckoning summer. Somewhere in between the harshness and the beauty.

Even in a difficult and specific time like that, when we were all trying to adapt to a strange and unsettled world, there was that feeling of expectancy that starts brimming at that time of year. Spring always brings with it a sense of renewal and possibility. The cherry blossoms, forsythia, and green haze seem to appear overnight and, like magic, color returns to a world that has been grey and cold for a long, long time.

You know that feeling, right?

It's a sense the light's returning.

Even in that season of new beginnings, I was not looking for him. I was not looking for *anyone*. I was the opposite of looking, actually, but there he was anyway. I'd seen him around a few times before. I noticed him because he's the sort of man you notice, but this was the first time I really *saw* him.

Handsome. Assured. *Great* smile. At ease. Comfortable in his own skin.

Obviously, I avoided him like the plague.

I did, however, begin referring to him as my crush, but only to people who wouldn't encounter him. Friends were thrilled–thrilled I even noticed someone. Thrilled there were signs I was coming back to life. My people are such good people. I was becoming more and more aware every day of how worried they'd been about me and for how long. I texted my friend Angela after the breakup and she later told me that she closed her eyes and said, "Thank God," when she read it. My cousin Mary told me that in that last year with James my light had gone out. I couldn't see it then, but I guess that's how it goes when you're in it. You simply acclimate to the darkness.

My friends asked me what my crush's name was. I told them I had no idea. They asked me what he was like. Same answer. One friend suggested I find out and I recoiled in horror. I said, *"Are you crazy? Why would I do such a thing? He is gorgeous, mute, and across the room. He is entirely theoretical. He's basically perfect right now."* I knew nothing about him other than the fact that he was very, very hard to ignore. Every once in a while we would catch each other's eye and smile. I assumed it was a coincidence, but he would tell me later that's because he was always looking at me.

I didn't want to meet him and I *certainly* didn't want to have a conversation. It tends to be with the talking that things go sideways. It's when they say the words. Then one Sunday I heard him talk. He got *more* attractive. What the hell.

A little later, he made his way over to me and we chatted for a few minutes. He introduced himself. His name was Shane. It was a nice day out and we both mentioned being excited to get outside and walk the boardwalk by the state beach. Then my friend Judy invited him out to breakfast with us. Treachery. He told me later he positioned himself to be asked.

Shane sat next to me at the large, round table in the back of a breakfast spot where a bunch of us met each week. It was a big group, but there was this gravitational pull between the two of us. I was incredibly aware of him the entire time. I had a hard time looking directly at him, so I looked at his hands a lot. I noticed that when someone talked he was fully present and gave them his complete attention, and when that someone was me it felt like the sun on my face. He asked me a lot of questions. He offered up some things, too. He seemed to want me to know him. There was something undeniable going on, some magnetic thing drawing us together–so naturally, at the conclusion of breakfast, I fled from the diner like I was being pursued by a bear.

The next week our breakfast group consisted of me and four of my girlfriends. And Shane. I don't even really know how that happened. I suspect Judy. Again, he was totally comfortable. That's a big thing and important to me. The women in my life are no joke and they are not negotiable.

That time, he walked me to my car, which was nowhere near his car. We chatted for about twenty minutes in the late February sunshine. Shane said he felt like there was an energy between us. He told me he'd thought about me a lot the previous week and that he was already looking forward to seeing me the following week. Didn't ask for my number, which I really liked, even though I 100% would have given it to him.

The next Sunday all my traitorous people were nowhere to be found. I was furious. This was not how I'd written the script. I wondered if in the absence of the group aspect he'd pass on breakfast. I wondered if I'd be brave enough to have breakfast with him without the buffer of my people. I did a lot of frantic thinking in a very short time. I was absurdly nervous and preemptively disappointed.

He came up to me with that megawatt smile and asked me where everyone was. When I shrugged he said, "*Well then, it looks like it's just you and me, kid. Let's go somewhere nice.*" It took me two very long seconds to decide to take the risk. "*Sounds good,*" I said.

We sat at brunch and talked for an hour and a half. We covered many of the things. I dragged it out as long as possible. My omelet came with couscous. I ate it one cous at a time. At the end of brunch, I felt a little forlorn. I did not want it to be over. He smiled that smile at me and said, "*I'm not ready to say goodbye to you. Will you come walk on the beach with me?*"

I said yes.

We went and walked the boardwalk in the sun on a beautiful day and talked and talked and talked. We talked about healing and growth and what it all meant to us. We talked about our families and our pasts, mistakes we made and lessons we learned and God and music.

Then he drove me back to my car. He said, "*I'm going to give you my card. No pressure. Call me, don't call me. Either way, I am looking forward to seeing you next Sunday.*"

He did not kiss me, which I liked–although I would 100% have kissed him back.

It was 1:00. I was tempted to text him before I pulled out of the parking lot, but I did not because I am super cool. I waited a few hours and went for a walk in the park. I sat on a bench in the late afternoon light and sent him a text thanking him for a lovely morning. He immediately texted back and said, "*What took you so long???? I have been waiting to hear from you all afternoon!*"

I spent an awful lot of time looking down at my phone and smiling in those early days.

The next day, I was walking Scout and talking to him on the phone and he said he had some places he wanted to show me, some walks he thought I would like. I said that sounded good and he said, "*It would be a date. You know that, right? Are you ready?*" It sounded like a genuine question, so I genuinely considered it.

I said yes.

He asked me if I liked surprises. I said I did as long as I knew what to wear. Might as well be authentically me from the very beginning, right? What's my outfit? He gave me just enough information to make clear he'd planned a whole day and that multiple footwear options would be necessary.

He told me we'd have breakfast, go for a nice walk in the woods and spend some time in a pretty country town. He asked if that was enough information.

Surprisingly, it was. I consulted Mary and Matt (obviously) and we came up with a sartorial game plan.

The next Sunday, on a bright gift of a day, we drove up north. He showed me places that were special to him. We talked and talked. We went to brunch at a quaint little place, sat by a window overlooking a half-frozen stream, and talked some more. He was friendly and gracious to the server. That's a big one for me. If you're not kind to people in the service industry, you are unkind.

A footwear change later found us on a trail in the cool, early spring afternoon. He asked whether I wanted to walk the complete loop or double back halfway. I asked him what the difference was and he said that the second half of the hike had more tree cover, so it would be darker and colder. I said I thought it would be fine and made the joke that I wasn't scared of the dark, but if he was, I'd hold his hand.

He looked at me–oh, how I would come to love the way he looks at me–smiled, and said, *"I think I want to hold your hand in the light."*

And so, he did.

He's a master craftsman and has the hands to prove it. Strong, rough, and capable. Holding his hand felt like the most natural thing in the world. He's the kind of man who puts you at ease because he just seems confident things will be fine. He's relentlessly positive. He's not trying to prove anything. He's just… happy. He's a man of faith and talks easily about God in a language that feels familiar–like home to me.

We went for ice cream and ate it shivering in the sunshine. We wandered through shops and galleries. We laughed and talked and teased each other. We talked about big things and ridiculous things. We held hands the whole time. Finally, seven hours later and much too soon, he drove me back to my car.

It was a perfect day.

When he dropped me back at my car, he kissed me. And I 100% kissed him back.

And then... COVID-19. Almost immediately after we began dating, he got the virus. He was so sick, just completely down for the count. I made a pot of chicken soup and brought it to him. I stood out on his deck and he stayed inside, sitting on the floor. So sick. So cute. I left the groceries and soup outside and drove away, wondering how long the shutdown would last and when I'd be able to see him again. I was afraid it might be weeks.

Then the gravity of what was happening settled on us and we realized normal dating would not be happening any time soon. I bemoaned the timing and he said, *"It'll make a great story someday."*

It was true. We could have looked at it as terrible, but, as with all things, it was entirely about perspective. In the absence of this forced separation, perhaps it would have been more heat and less light. It felt as though God pumped the brakes for us. Slowed things down. Instead of racing around, going and doing, we spent hours and hours on the phone, talking and being.

We went for a hike a couple of months into the shutdown. We picked an arduous trail where it would be less crowded and social distancing would be easier. He patiently waited when I crouched to examine moss and admire mushrooms and smiled at me as I noticed and photographed the moments as they unfolded. He tends to look straight ahead, and I tend to look up and down. He helps me see important things right in front of me, and perhaps I help him see beauty he might otherwise miss.

We came upon a tunnel carved out of a hill. As we approached, the entrance looked foreboding. We walked through and he shined his phone upward so we could try and see the bats that roost there. As we came near the end, the opening to exit was luminous in a way you can only truly appreciate if you are leaving deep darkness.

Together, hands clasped, we stepped back into the bright afternoon.

Farther down the trail, he gestured at a log down by the bank of the river and asked me if I wanted rest for a minute.

I said yes.

The sun moved behind some clouds. The temporary grey was soothing, in a way. Contemplative. We sat a while under the steepled pines and listened to the water rush by us. He meditated for a bit. I prayed. One of us talking to God, one of us listening.

We were still and it was quiet. The sun eased out the other side of the cloud bank, and it was good. I turned my face toward it. I said yes to warmth and light. I said yes to happiness and fun. I said yes to connection and adventure and possibility. And risk. Of course.

Yes.

Yes.

Yes

Chapter Eight
Boxes

Less than a week after my relationship with James ended, I needed to head back to his house to get some more things. I was out of my mind when I packed and the random contents of my suitcase bore that out. He was away on business, so I took the opportunity to have the house to myself while I began to sift through the flotsam and jetsam of our shipwrecked life to assemble a starter kit to rebuild mine. When I walked into the house, I immediately noticed that every single picture that contained me, my kids–even my dog–had been removed from the walls, the mantel, and his office. History was already being re-written to be *his* story, with select chapters brutally excised.

I remembered how much it meant to me that our whole families were represented on our gallery wall. His ex and mine. My kids and his. Both dogs. Back when his boys were young enough to have a playroom, there was a whiteboard in it that had house rules written by their mom before the divorce. He asked me if it bothered me that it was still there. I told him it was my favorite thing about the room. I loved that he wanted to keep it there. It made perfect sense to me. We were going to be that modern family. I really believed it.

In the center of the gallery wall was a photograph I took of the ramp leading down to the dock near his family's house in Maine. I guess he figured it was his. Looking at the collage, I realized that I'd taken and/or framed the overwhelming majority of the photos there–even the ones of his family. He'd only taken down the ones that contained me and mine, though. He seemed happy enough to keep what I brought to his life, he just wanted me out of it. It felt deliberately mean.

I walked through the house looking at all the things I'd done to make it feel like a home. The kitchen where I'd cooked dinner every night. The dining room where I'd helped the boys with schoolwork. The art on the walls, the lamps, the pillows. The family photos, the furniture.

Yeah, I don't think so. It's your house, but it was me that made it a home. It wasn't dead when I left, it was dead when I got here. You don't get to keep what I brought to this. You want me gone? You got it.

I was like the fucking Grinch. *Oh, did I bring that refrigerator lightbulb? I'll be taking that.* Everything remotely feasible to bring with me to whatever new life I might cobble together felt urgent. The only exceptions were things for the boys. I left my TV. What was I going to do with a 60-inch screen? Take up Fortnight?

I thought about all the times I helped the boys with school projects. I left boxes of art supplies. They always used my printer more than I did, and where would I put it, anyway? And the things I couldn't bring because they didn't fit my life anymore–like my beautiful dining room table with room for ten, the chest freezer in the garage that could fit enough food for a whole family–were particularly painful to leave behind

I stepped out onto the deck. A few years back, he'd installed a pergola. One night, when we were out for dinner on James' birthday, his youngest called it a Portugal, so from then on, of course, so did I. Underneath the Portugal was all of the furniture I bought James for father's day the previous year. It was such a pretty spot. I thought back to one particular night when he and I sat out there listening to music. He'd put strings of market lights around the perimeter because he knew how much I loved them. We both swung in the hammocks he'd hung, and the dogs lay at our feet while we played songs for each other and talked. It felt easy, like it used to. It was during a tough stretch, but that particular night things were good. We could see each other. We could hear each other. I remember thinking, *This is who we really are. This is us.*

Standing on the deck, I had the realization I'd never sit out there again on a summer morning with my coffee. I wouldn't hunt through the vines in the garden searching for the season's last cherry tomatoes, still warm from the sun. I wouldn't smile listening to the neighbors' kids shriek in their pool. I shook my head hard, as though to dislodge the memories. Remembering the hard times wasn't pleasant, but it somehow hurt less.

Out in the garage was my freezer. I remembered getting it back when I was married. It was such a big deal to me. We had an extra fridge and a chest freezer in the garage. Like rich people. We had a Costco membership. Like grown-ups. When I stocked the freezer and the pantry I felt safe. There was something about the feeling of plenty and preparedness that felt like what I imagined home to be. It was hard to leave the freezer behind, but it's one of those things that makes sense for a family. And I was not a family.

James texted me when he got back to the house after I was done. He expressed his shock. I'm not sure what he thought was going to happen. Maybe I would just leave and take my sweaters? When you've built a life together, there is no cleaving without loss on both sides, even if one person makes the decision. I'd had my whole life turned upside down, and he was taken aback by the absence of some home decor.

Moving day finally arrived. It was a bright, chilly November morning. James had cleared out, and my crew of hooligans arrived, en masse. My friend Johnny went and got the U-Haul. My God, how people showed up for me. They were all wise-cracking and upbeat, but fiercely and sweetly protective. During that awful time I went to a 7:00 recovery meeting every morning. I could fake it almost everywhere else, but not in that church basement and not with those people. In that church basement, I was undone and those people let me be. I feel lucky to be in recovery. The price of admission to that community is to tell the truth about your life. That simple, hard thing gets you a seat in a circle of busted-up folding chairs filled with people who will have your back relentlessly, forever.

James left a note on the kitchen counter letting me know I could use the storage unit for as long as I needed to, along with a check for the furniture he was buying from me that was more generous than it needed to be. He was trying to be decent. I really do believe that. In his note he encouraged Mary to *"keep on loving"* me. I'm sure his intentions were good, but when Mary saw it she let out an impressive string of expletives. I wouldn't have thought I could laugh that day, but hearing my elegant cousin swear like a sailor on leave was oddly therapeutic. It was helpful to have people angry on my behalf. I couldn't summon it.

I led my motley crew through the rooms showing them which furniture was mine, which boxes were to be packed on the truck, and which ones James had agreed to donate for me. The finality of it began to settle in and I started to get overwhelmed and teary. Mary looked at me and a steely expression came over her beautiful face. She made eye contact with the guys and said, *"She's done here."* She handed me my keys and told me they would meet me at my new place. *"I've got this,"* she said. I nodded. I knew she did. Mary's a force of nature. I walked out to my car, parked on the street like a guest at the house I used to call home, got in and put my forehead on the cold steering wheel.

Okay, I thought. *Okay.*

I deliberately drove out a different way to avoid going past the beach. As I merged onto I-95 headed toward my new city, I turned the radio on. Almost immediately, familiar guitar chords and Billy Joe Armstrong's voice filled the car, singing about turning points and forks in the road. "*You have got to be fucking kidding me,*" I said to the universe. I could have changed the station, I guess, but instead I rolled down the windows and turned the volume all the way up.

I pulled into the parking lot of my apartment building. It was so strange to think it was where I would sleep that night. I rode the elevator up to the top floor and walked down the narrow window-lined hallway. I turned my key in the lock, opened the door, and stepped into my new life. The apartment, with its cathedral ceilings and gleaming wood floors, seemed cheerful and welcoming. And unfamiliar. And empty. And quiet. My car was crammed with boxes and bags, but I only carried one thing under my arm. The yellow sign that made a promise I still needed to believe in. Love wins.

Okay.

Months later, in early summer, James reached out to me to say I needed to get the remainder of my things out of the storage unit. It was the last, fraying string in the connection between us, and it needed to be severed. I knew it, even wanted it by that time, but I felt low-key dread the entire week leading up to it. There's something about finality that's just so damned sad. I reminded him that he still had some of my camping things, plus I needed to get the keys to the unit, so I made arrangements to meet him at the house.

He was in his car in the driveway when I got there. We were polite. He told me to take the time I needed and to text him when I left, because he was going to take the boys out to eat. He didn't owe me that unnecessary detail, but at least it hurt. I went into the garage. I felt disoriented. It was like being at a natural history museum and looking at a diorama of where I used to live. Almost real, but not quite. I half-heartedly looked through some boxes for my lanterns and gear, to no avail.

James previously told me all my remaining things had been moved to storage, but standing in the driveway he said there was some stuff in the basement. My Christmas boxes were all still downstairs. Perfect. It's not like holiday stuff has any emotion attached to it.

I braced myself to walk into the house. As soon as I stepped inside, I saw that Bad Dog and Blu were in the kennel together. Both dogs were coming unglued with happiness. I had not prepared for this. I let them out, scooped Bad Dog up, and buried my face in the curly fur of his neck. He licked me incessantly, so much so that it took me a minute to realize I was crying. I put him down and grabbed Blu's massive head like I always did. He was an enormous beast, but so sweet. Always really sweet. I kissed him on the snout, and picked up my little Baddie again. I hadn't let myself feel this part. Jesus.

I spent a few minutes with them and then put them back in the crate.

I walked down the stairs to the basement and began pulling my boxes out of the recessed storage area. I mentally thanked myself for never combining our holiday decorations, and then wondered about that for a minute. All those years in, it would have made much more sense to pack them all together, and yet there my boxes were, with my name on them.

As my friend Matt would say, *That's interesting.* Looking back, it's probably a detail I'd have avoided telling Matt, if for no other reason than his intuitive Spidey-senses would have been all over it.

My friend Matt is my touchstone. Our wiring and our histories are so similar, and ever since we met in the comment section of my blog years earlier we've been two peas in a pod. He's also a survivor of childhood trauma and is in recovery. We're both ENFPs and Enneagram 2s. He and I are basically the same human. We have a kind of spiritual shorthand with each other. The closest we get to disagreeing is saying, *"Say more about that..."* in the unlikely event we don't get what the other is saying right away. He is more than a friend. He has become my brother, and is usually my first call when anything big or hard or amazing happens. We have the kind of relationship where we tell each other the truth, no matter what. That made him an invaluable resource and a devastating mirror.

I hauled everything upstairs. I walked over to the crate and kissed each dog's snout, knowing it would be for the last time. Bad Dog whined so piteously, I wondered if he knew it too. I thought about letting him out again, but knew it would only get harder. I stepped back into the garage and looked around. I glanced down at the tangle of shoes and sports equipment that used to trip me regularly. I didn't think I could miss piles of boys' grubby sneakers and flip flops, but I was wrong. Their feet were bigger than when I left. They were growing without me.

I packed the Christmas boxes into the back seat of my car and drove down to the beach. His beach. I sat watching the gulls swoop and cry, and thought how strange it is that we bind and cleave with people throughout our lives. We love people and don't want to imagine life without them, almost cannot picture ourselves in their absence, but then we have to, so we do and we can. But not our same lives and not our same selves. There were parts of me that stayed behind. They needed to. The woman I was becoming was different from the woman who was so starved in her relationship she convinced herself that the crumbs of a rare night of peace and lights and music were a feast. And maybe the space created in my life by the removal, however brutal, of people, places, and things I loved, was creating room for something new. Someone new. Me.

———

The following weekend, Shane and I went to tackle the storage unit. We'd only been together for a few months, so I was a little anxious about doing such an emotionally loaded thing with him. He wanted to help, though, and had a truck, so I accepted the offer. When I unlocked the padlock on the door and swung it open, I felt a wave of dread at the sight that greeted me. In addition to the boxes I'd expected, all of the stuff James said he would donate for me was stashed there. I'd been prepared for this to be quick and easy and that was not going to happen. I was completely overwhelmed. I can do impossible things like a champ, but easy-to-moderate ones sometimes paralyze me.

I think Shane sensed that I was about to melt down. Luckily, he is extremely linear and logical, so his methodical brain kicked into high gear. *"Okay, sweetheart. What's next? What do you need?"*

We started the grueling task of sorting out the boxes and bags to be donated from the ones I would be moving to a new storage unit. I gave myself a talking to.

No feelings, Laura. Put 'em on a shelf. Get your act together. Just get this done. This is just stuff.

Then I saw it.

Oh, Jesus. No. Oh, shit. Shit, shit, shit.

Maybe I can ignore it. I tried to keep sorting things, with the large, flat, brown cardboard box marked 'Master Bedroom,' sitting there like a bomb. It looked innocuous enough, but I knew the contents were explosive. What's the TSA slogan? If you see something, say something?

While I was trying to decide what to do, Shane picked it up.

"What's this?"

I froze.

Inside that box was the wedding dress I bought back when I thought the inevitable trajectory of my relationship with James would involve us getting married. I'd envisioned the whole thing. I'd seen the dress online and it was so simple and romantic. Strapless silk with a ruffle cascading down the front. James always loved me in white. The dress was 50% off and I couldn't resist. I only tried it on once. It was perfect. Then I packed it away thinking that when the time came, I could surprise him with the fact that I'd been so certain about our future, I already had the dress. I was always writing the sweetest story of us, and the neat thing about stories is they don't need facts to support them.

I was humiliated. I considered not admitting the truth of what the box contained. Shane and I had only been together about four months at that point. How much truth was too truthy? Then I remembered that I'd made a promise to myself to be fully authentic in this new relationship, no matter what. I had to believe it would be better for him to not love the actual woman in front of him than to have the woman he loved actually be an illusion. So I flipped shame off and said,

"That's the wedding dress I bought back when I thought James and I would get married."

He stopped in his tracks and looked at me. It was a very quiet, exceedingly long few seconds before he spoke again. I could tell whatever he'd expected me to say, that was not it. Fair.

"Really?" he said.

"Yep. Really."

"What do you want to do with it? Sell it?"

"Nope. Donate. Someone at Goodwill is going to seriously score."

Shane tried to make light of it. *"You don't want to save it for our wedding, someday?"*

"No. That's not my dress."

We continued to sort through things like all of this was normal. I kept thinking about that meme I love–you know, the one with the little dog sitting at the table drinking a cup of coffee, completely surrounded by fires, with the caption, *This is fine.*

Once we finished identifying which boxes I was getting rid of, we loaded them into the back of his truck and headed up the street to drop them off. Standing outside the Goodwill donation center, stacking all of the stuff in the bin, Shane picked the box containing the dress up and hesitated before putting it in. *"You're sure?"*

"Yes. "

I climbed up into the truck. We headed back to the unit to grab the remaining things. He seemed to know I didn't feel like talking. I was grateful. When the last box was placed on the perfectly loaded dolly, we stood in the door of the now mostly vacant unit. Shane put his hands gently on my shoulders. I looked up into his eyes and said,

"Thank you so much for helping."

He said,

"You're welcome, sweetheart. Now we're going to say a prayer for him."

My throat constricted and my eyes stung. I nodded. We stood silently in the door of the unit, between the near-empty past and the partly-full future. I remembered what a friend counseled me to do in early recovery when I was struggling with a difficult relationship that needed healing. She said, *"I want you to pray for her to have everything you would want for yourself and more."* So I did. I prayed for James' health and happiness. I prayed for his joy and healing and peace. And I prayed for love. I wanted love and I wanted him to have it, too. Whatever that looked like. I raised my head and met Shane's gaze. He smiled at me.

"Now, slam the door."

And so, I did.

Chapter Nine
Fortress

One late summer morning, Shane and I went back to the restaurant where we had our first date. Back then, it was barely spring and chilly. We sat inside, him looking at me and me looking out at the partially thawed stream trickling past, while my hands fidgeted relentlessly with the napkin in my lap. This time, we sat outside on the deck. We held hands as we both watched the torrent of water rush by as the sunlight coming through the leaves made patterns on the deck. I looked into the face I'd come to know so well, and met the gaze my nerves had me studiously avoiding that first day.

"I think I'm the one who is guarded in this relationship."

His gorgeous blue eyes crinkled up at the corners as he smiled that smile at me. Not like it was funny—well, maybe a *little* like it was funny. This did not appear to be brand new information for him the way it was for me. It was more like he'd been waiting for me to know it, too. Like he was glad we finally both knew it so we could work through it. That's the way he is. *Here is the thing. Let's look at it squarely and talk it out calmly.* It's bizarre.

So, it was one of those unforgivably obvious things and, once acknowledged, I couldn't un-know it. I thought about it every day. I talked to my people about it. Matt mostly, because he always gets it. He always gets everything. Not just in the *I understand* way, but in the, *Oooh, YEP* way.

Thank you, God, for Matt.

I came to realize the walls around my heart by way of our vacation to the West Coast. We'd just returned and I needed to quarantine for two weeks for work, which would have us together for three weeks straight–which, we can all agree, is SO MANY DAYS. Anyway, I'd be at his place. I had all my vacation clothes and all my work clothes for the next stretch. I was trying to organize it all in a way that made sense in my bags and he said,

"Would you like a drawer in the dresser?"

He'd barely said it, and just like Harry says in *When Harry Met Sally*, the words were just HANGING there, like in a cartoon bubble.

"No. No. No. NO. Nooooo, that's okay. It's fine. This is fine. I'm fine. I'll figure it out. I mean, thank you. But, no. Uh-uh. Nope."

He chuckled quietly and said, *"So, that's a no, then."*

I vamoosed into the bedroom to Jenga my belongings in such a way that they would take up as little real estate as possible, and be in a state of already packed and halfway out the door. You know. Just in case.

I texted Matt immediately and informed him that I am a massive jerk.

I'd talked this through a lot with him. My fears, my hesitance, my state of readiness–the way I seemed to be keeping one eye on the door at all times. I was like an emotional doomsday prepper. Quick to perceive threats, ready to go underground, primed for the worst case scenario.

Here's the thing about love: it never comes without risk. Ever. Anything and anyone outside of you can be taken away. And likely will be, at some point, in some form or fashion. And the more you love, the more you invest, the greater the loss if and when it happens.

There were some losses associated with the demise of my previous relationship which I still could not think about without coming undone. Overnight I lost my home, the kids I helped raise, my pets, my favorite place on earth, and my partner of seven years, my friend of more than thirty. To this day, it is *still* shocking to me. My initial feeling, once I got up off the floor, was that I did not ever want to put myself in a position to be hurt like that again. That I would rather be alone forever than give someone else the power to harm me that way.

For a while, there were some aspects of what happened which I simply wouldn't let myself think about. It's a gift born of trauma, actually. The ability to put shit on a shelf. I can compartmentalize like a boss, right up until I can't. It's only ever a temporary strategy. It's pain on layaway. I knew full well I would have to pay the balance at some point, and there'd be interest accrued for having waited. It felt like it was time to maybe get some help with it. I'll be honest, though, I was so tired of healing. Well, it's probably more accurate to say I was sick to death of needing to heal. I was sick to death of doing *work*. The problem with that was, I wanted to travel light. I was tired of the weight of the anger and grief and fear that seemed to insert themselves into things when I least expected it.

Doing the work to heal was the only way to be free to really love wholeheartedly. It took me a while to get to a place where that even seemed like a worthy goal again. I was hesitant to meet Shane's kids early on, not because I was nervous we wouldn't like each other, but because I was sure we would. I was afraid I would love them. It would just be more to lose. I did my level best to keep him and them at bay. And then I met them, and now I love them. Because, of course I do. And so, I had to decide whether I wanted to keep my heart safe or use it as intended.

It's like people who skydive. When I see footage of them perched on the edge of the door of the plane, I wonder how it is they will themselves to do something that every survival instinct we have, codified in our very DNA since the beginning of time, must balk at. How is it that you come to the decision to fling yourself into the vast and bottomless sky? Or like our primordial ancestors, who dragged themselves out of the ocean in a quest to evolve. They left the relative safety of the only environment they'd ever known to grow into what they were meant to become. It's counterintuitive at a cellular level.

Massive risk, certain hardship, wild discomfort. I guess that's the cost of a new life, but only every single time. How fun. What a terrific system.

I'm an early morning person by nature, frequently rising before 5:00 a.m. I'd snap the leash on Scout pre-dawn, at what my friends call 'stupid o'clock.' I am always seeking to improve my conscious contact with Dog, as I understand Her. We typically had the park to ourselves. Even the squirrels were still sleeping, much to Scout's dismay. One day, though, we ran into a young woman jogging. She exclaimed how cute Scout was, jumping up and clawing the tree, as though it was a critter vending machine. She made a joke about how her dog just wants to be friends with the squirrels. I said, *"Mine doesn't. She wants to eat them. All of them."* She laughed and I smiled. Hahaha.

But it's true.

Scout was, as my grandmother would have said, living the life of Riley. She was adored and well-fed. She routinely ate better than a lot of humans I know. Every need she had was met and then some, but that's not how her life started off. Scout was a stray. The first time Shane met her, a month or so after we started dating, he fed her a piece of perfectly cooked fish from his plate. He marveled, *"She likes it!"* Um, yeah, dude. She was feral less than a year ago. She ate trash. Does she like salmon? She sure does.

She was safe and spoiled. She finally had a home where she was adored and indulged. I was not going anywhere. Still, that's not the story she lived out of. When you come from real scarcity, it's hard to trust abundance. When you've not been able to count on another being to have your back or meet your needs, you learn to rely solely on yourself. When you are accustomed to there being no soft place to fall, you walk around braced for hardness.

When you've been harmed, you expect harm.

I occasionally posted on social media about my early morning city jaunts with Scout, and many people expressed concern about my safety. I had one reader frame it in a way that got me thinking. I said something about being mindful of where I go and aware of my surroundings and she said, *"Yes, but do you FEEL safe?"* My knee-jerk response to that was, *"I guess, not that it really matters."*

The morning of the day James ended things, I woke up feeling secure that I was part of a family and had a home. Even though things were hard, I did not doubt that he loved and was committed to me. When I put my head on the pillow that evening, I knew that had been an illusion. As it turns out, *feeling* safe is not safety, so it did not feel safe to feel safe anymore. The smart thing, the prepared thing, seemed to be constantly living on guard, waiting for the other shoe to drop. I didn't even really believe in *safe* anymore. I looked back on times in my marriage and my relationship with James when I felt safe and loved, and I felt like a sucker. I was afraid to love again, even though it was obvious to anyone paying attention that it was too late.

The thing about being feral is you understand safety is a feeling, not a fact. You know that while you may be in a moment of comfort or plenty, it can all go away without warning, so staying in survival mode seems not only wise, but necessary.

Scout was pretty sure I'd feed her, but she was also perfectly ready to have to fend for herself at any given moment, thankyouverymuch. I once saw a meme about how ultra-independence is a trauma response. It sure is. That and its good buddy, hypervigilance.

The only solution seemed to be time and grace. A relationship I'd treasured and believed would last forever was thrown away, like so much garbage. I'll likely never understand having an off-switch like that, which is fine. There are things worth understanding and that is not one of them. I didn't even really want to be someone who could understand that.

Several months later, Matt visited me. He was going through his own grief over a breakup he'd not seen coming. When he suggested coming to New Haven, in *my* head it was because he was considering moving there and being my kooky next door neighbor. Rhoda to my Mary. Kramer to my Jerry. Grace to my Will. I figured we could have slumber parties and he could sign off on my outfit every morning, the way God intended.

We'd come back from walking Scout through the Yale campus downtown, and were sitting in a little cafe about two blocks from my building. Matt was working on his manuscript, which he'd tried to do in my apartment, but Scout's incessant attempts to divert his attention by unceremoniously dropping her tennis ball on his laptop as he tried to type seemed to indicate the need for a location change. I drank coffee and enjoyed watching the cute servers try to catch Matt's eye. Flirting with masks on presents a challenge, but I'm here to tell you–it can be done

We were talking about his breakup and my walls. We're so much fun, I swear. I was talking about saying the words *"I love you"* and how they didn't really mean anything to me anymore. And how I didn't even know what being IN love meant. Basically, romantic love was bullshit. That was the Cliff Notes version. Matt laughed incredulously, then looked at me and said, *"LAURA."* the way only he can. I looked up from my coffee into one of my favorite faces in the world. He looked stricken. He said, *"God, that's just the worst thing I've ever heard. That is, like, awful."*

All of a sudden, I heard my defensive chatter through his ears. I heard how my guarded justification for keeping love at bay was received by this person who had come to be one of the most valued and wise sounding boards in my life. I had one of my best friends, maybe the person in the whole world who is most like me, mirror my fear back at me.

It was painful and sad. But also good, you know? We can't change what we refuse to acknowledge. If I was going to let cynicism turn me into a coward, then I would get the relationship I deserved.

This relationship, not even a year old, was worth fighting for. I was trying to trust Shane–but it wasn't even really about that. Truth be told, Shane had very little to do with it. I was trying to trust *me*. He kept joking about removing bricks from the wall, but ultimately he couldn't. Not because he wasn't reliable (he was) or deeply good (he was) or didn't want to (I believed he did) He couldn't do it because it simply was not his job, and we can all only do our own work. It was mine. Well, me and God. It was our work.

One day during the first month I had Scout, I got held up at work and was gone for a longer stretch than usual. I came home and she'd gotten a hold of a pair of my glasses and destroyed them. She lost her mind when I walked in the door. Half mad at me, half overjoyed I was back. She wasn't sure of me yet. She wasn't healed from previous mistreatment. We were still learning how to love one another. Ten months later, when I was gone for that same length of time, she would barely lift her head when I walked in. She'd just lie there, tail thumping in happiness. She was glad I was back, but she kind of figured I would be. She was surer.

Maybe I would be, too.

Chapter Ten
Island

From time to time, when I am feeling nostalgic or decide to engage in a little emotional cutting, I'll scroll through Facebook Memories. It can be a wonderful feature. It can highlight how far I've come, remind me of incredible experiences, and serve as a digital scrapbook for where I was on a given day in a given year. For someone grieving, however, it is a goddamned minefield. I avoided it for a long time, but the summer after James and I split, I decided to risk it. The first picture that came up was of the island. Not surprising. I always wrote in real time about what it was like to be there. I loved it so much and part of my joy was sharing it.

James's family has a farm on an island just off the gorgeous, unforgiving coast of Maine. A little strip of heaven fourteen miles long and one and-a-half miles across its widest. Their house is perched on the highest point and is surrounded by acre upon acre of meadow and woods. We went there every year, for a week or two. It was their family summer home. It wasn't mine, but my heart didn't know that.

I remember how excited he was to share it with me that first year. We got to the ferry, parked in line, and walked down to the beach. The back of the truck was loaded with food and supplies piled up to the roof. James had a whole system, perfected after decades of such trips. *"It's expensive to get groceries once you're there, and they won't have everything,"* he said. That's the nature of islands, I guess. They won't have everything you need, and even if they do, it'll cost you. I smiled because he was both talking it up and managing my expectations. He told me there were no restaurants. Really no shopping. No "beachy" beaches. I wondered what we'd do, but I didn't really care. I only wanted to be with him.

When it was time to board, we got back in the SUV and let ourselves be guided onto the ferry by a man with a face like a barnacle. He impatiently pointed at a parking spot the laws of physics seem to preclude us fitting into. He kept motioning James to creep up farther and farther, until finally he gave the 'stop' sign. I found it oddly stressful, but James didn't. He just always seemed to assume there would be enough space for him. Finally, the ferry embarked on the twenty-minute trip. I could see his broad shoulders relax. His face began to look younger, somehow. I wondered at the power of a place to have that effect on someone. We had the windows rolled down, the music cranked up, and the smell of the ocean did what it always has done for me–I breathed deeper, slower, easier. I looked out at the water, where every so often I'd see a seal head pop up in the harbor, slick and curious.

The drive from the dock to the farm backed up his statements about island life. Two little markets. One gas pump. Lots of trees. Farmhouses, old weathered barns, and grey-shingled cottages with riotous gardens overrun with leggy, cerulean hydrangeas. Plenty of extravagant homes, too, but in true Maine fashion, they were tucked away down private roads. There were no traffic lights and very few cars, but every vehicle we passed engaged in the long-standing tradition of the two-fingered salute off the steering wheel.

The farm had been in his family since the 1940s. His mother's aunt and uncle purchased it at the same time several of their friends bought homes there. That place was always about togetherness and connection.

We came around a bend in the road, turned into the driveway, and began to make our way up the dirt road to the house. James stopped the truck to let the boys out, so they could run up the hill. Banked on either side by wildflowers and blueberry bushes, the drive was steep enough that you couldn't see the farm until you were right in front of it. The house was white with black shutters, and kitty-corner to it was a big barn, a sun-faded red. Behind it stretched acres of rippling tall grass, with a path mowed down the middle. Beyond the meadow, just visible above the crest of pines, was the glittering water of Penobscot Bay.

I instantly understood the draw, why James couldn't wait to get there, why he couldn't wait to share it. It felt both familiar and new, and suspended in time.

For a long time, I was certain we would be married there. I was sure of it. It seems ridiculous now. Embarrassing. So many times I imagined walking down that aisle of grass, with James waiting for me in the clearing that overlooked the ocean. I knew what song would play as I made my way through our family and friends–a big, laid-back gathering of everyone who loved us, all of whom would be overjoyed at our happiness. I could see it. I guess I was so sure we'd get there, it didn't occur to me we never really talked about it.

The house was beautiful–old, and quirky with narrow, steep staircases, peeling wallpaper, and family photos everywhere. One room meandered into another, filled with evidence of lives well-lived and families well-loved. Nothing showy about it. It was a home that, in the words of the old Irish blessing, rose up to meet you when you entered.

Outside, the barn served as home base for all things fun. There was a ramp in front, which was put to good use by James's boys, who I'd nicknamed Thing One and Littlest, and their cousins, on bikes they'd long outgrown. The boys generally turned wild on the third day there after the device detox and the attendant wailing,

moaning, and negotiating had passed. Littlest would hunt snakes for
hours. He named the big, red one El Diablo, and most of the rest of
them, Roger. That kid. He delighted in keeping them in coolers
where they would serve as a terrifying surprise for whoever went in
search of a cold drink. Thing One would tear around the landing
strip on his bike, and, in the time-honored tradition of big brothers,
torment his younger sibling.

Just inside the barn door, an old transistor radio perched on
one of the shelves, perfect for classic rock, country, and Red Sox
games—all things that sound better with a little static. One wall was
covered in license plates from all over. The barn's interior housed
fishing gear, farm equipment, bicycles, tools, a shuffleboard table,
the requisite beer fridge, and the recreational detritus accumulated
by generations of summer vacationers.

We settled into a rhythm right away. I'd never felt so at ease so
quickly. It was less like discovering a place and more like remembering
one. Days were mostly spent outside, and evenings would find us in
the breezeway, an addition built on to the house. It was warm and
inviting, with a fireplace and lots of windows on both sides. Hanging
high on the pine paneled walls were two deer heads. They were
mainlanders–I believe they came from Pennsylvania. I typically don't
love seeing animal noggins mounted as decoration, but there was
something endearing about those two perpetual onlookers. The
boys were always naming them. The last summer I was there they
were dubbed Dave and Buster.

To the left of the hearth there was a big tin cabinet filled with
well-worn board games and puzzles. Every night we'd have a fire,
and the rickety table would play host to rounds of Pictionary or
Apples to Apples, or, as the kids got a little older, cards. James and
I would play epic games of what he deemed Rummy 100,000. He'd
keep upping the ceiling until he won a game. There was a
serendipity to sitting across from him, the two of us competing and
teasing one another. Thirty years ago, the games had involved
quarters and beer, and while much had changed, the trash talk was

still merciless. We'd known each other since we were teenagers, and now we sat there, each with kids of our own, having found one another again. It was hard to remember not knowing him.

One of my first nights on the island, I was cleaning up after dinner. Slowing down and being still had always been really difficult for me, and before I got sober I was perpetually in hustle mode, trying to prove how indispensable I was. I was puttering around the kitchen when James called from the front porch, "*Babe, come here.*"

"*In a minute,*" I responded, busy putting things away.

His deep voice filtered in, "*No, babe. Now.*"

I sighed. The screen door creaked as I stepped out onto the small deck off the kitchen into the inky Maine night.

"*Sit down,*" he said. I probably rolled my eyes. I remember being exasperated.

"*Look up,*" he said.

I grudgingly sat down on the steps, tilted my head back, and gasped. He draped an arm over my shoulders and I began to cry. Until that moment, I'd always thought of van Gogh's *The Starry Night* as fantastical–but there it was. Everything around me slowed down. The sky was a shade of blue-black I'd never seen before, and the stars… How were there so many? They seemed closer than the fireflies that had blinked in the meadow earlier at dusk. And the Milky Way… It's an actual thing, you know. I shook my head almost angrily. He'd known me since I was a girl. He knew how I felt about crying. He took my hand, looked at me, and smiled.

"*I know,*" he said.

I know all the scientific reasons for why the sky above that island is what it is. I can tell you about weather patterns and the absence of light pollution. The real answer, though, the one that feels true in my heart, is that particular stretch of land is just a little closer to heaven.

That night we climbed the steep, impossibly narrow staircase and fell into bed between sheets that had been washed and hung on the line so many times you could practically see through them. I slept through the night, which was rare for me before I got sober. I woke up before sunrise, with a headache–because before I stopped drinking I woke up every morning with a headache–but rested. I started to pull the covers back to get up, but James threw an arm over me and said, "*Stay.*" I did, for a while, and looked out the window at the wall of fog that had rolled in overnight. Once I knew he was back asleep, I eased out of the bed carefully, so as not to wake him, and headed downstairs to write. I was eager to have some time alone, just the island and me.

Our days fell into an easy rhythm and the week was over far too soon. When it came time to leave, I cried again. It meant something to him that I loved it the way I did. At least, I think so. I don't know.

———

When we returned the next summer, I was sober–though just barely. It had been a really hard year, and the last six months before I'd stopped drinking had been catastrophic. There's just no other word for it. Hard on me, exponentially harder on those who loved me. I was exhausted and anxious and in need of a place to heal. Early sobriety is uncomfortable and scary on its best day, so while I was grateful to be sober, I was nervous to head to a place where there were no recovery meetings. I wasn't sure I could go and not drink. How would I hang out in the barn and not have a beer? What would sunset out on the lawn be without a glass of wine? I worried incessantly leading up to the trip, but I never considered not going. The irresistible pull of the island was already at work, so I loaded my phone up with the numbers of sober people I'd met and made the six-hour drive north. This time, I knew where I was headed. This time it felt like going home.

In the truck on the way, James asked, "*What are you most excited for in Maine?*" I quickly rattled off a dozen things. "*What are you most excited for?*" I countered. "*Just to get you there,*" he said. "*Just to bring you to the place you love.*"

The island felt different. I wasn't drunk at night and I wasn't hungover in the morning, so I fell asleep easily and woke with a clear head and a happy heart. Even far away from my meetings, I experienced less anxiety about trying to not drink there. I could feel the magic settling in. I could breathe easier. I could be still. Ann Voskamp captured it perfectly when she wrote, "*Life is so urgent it necessitates living slow.*" The only pressure I felt was to soak it all up– to make the most of the experience, even if that meant doing very little. I noticed I didn't feel the need to constantly be productive. I slept better, I ate more. I spent more time outside. And I wrote. I wrote and wrote and wrote. It was as though my fingers couldn't keep up with the stories pouring out of me.

As raucous as the breezeway was at night, in the morning it was a sanctuary. I would wake before the sun rose and wrap myself up in a heavy sweater, because even the hottest days on-island gave way to chilly nights, perfect for sleeping. I'd tiptoe down the creaky stairs and turn on the coffee. While I waited for it to brew, I'd stand at the picture window in front of the kitchen sink and try to peer through the mist. It's funny how things can be right before your eyes and invisible. I'd squint, trying to make out anything beyond the wall of vapor rising off the field, which seemed to catch and hold the buttery yellow morning sun. Then, as if conjured, there'd be a deer. Then two. Suddenly visible. A moment before, there was nothing there but grass and light, and then, out of nowhere, things directly in front of me became clear.

James had a big, extended family. Imperfect, as all families are– but a family that showed up for each other in a way I was starved for. His was a family that prioritized togetherness. I was so desperate to be a part of that again. Even my relationships that had begun to heal were still fragile, and we were all being careful with one another. There was none of that with James's family. There were endless funny stories told at each other's expense, reminiscing about childhood and summers past. I missed having inside jokes and nonsensical traditions. Those are the things that make a family *your* family. The '*I don't know why we have to watch* Muppet Christmas Carol *right after the Thanksgiving dishes are done, but we do.*' sort of thing. Those rhythms and oddities are the fingerprints of belonging.

It's likely why I was so obsessed with the show *Parenthood*. I wanted to be part of a family that laughed and played and ate and fought and struggled together. They drove each other crazy because they knew each other. They weren't precious with one another. They lived out loud and up close. I talked about it so much that my friend Lisa photoshopped me into the outdoor dining room at Zeke and Camille's house. She tucked me in between Lauren Graham and Peter Krause at the long table under the market lights–an honorary Braverman.

I wanted to be absorbed into James's big, messy, loving family. Part of the appeal was likely that relationships with my own family of origin were still so broken. I'd done so much damage–there was hurt and mistrust and resentment. I'd only just begun to do the work to repair what I could, and I felt deeply disconnected as a result, so I took to his family's traditions with the zeal you only ever see in a convert. One such tradition was going to get ice cream every day at 4:00. Yes, before dinner. I was downright militant about enforcing the rule–and I don't really eat ice cream. I did on the island, though.

We'd spend the afternoon lounging in the sun on the dock, and, when we were hot enough, diving into water so cold it seemed to suck the oxygen from our lungs. The boys would run and shriek, daring each other to cannonball off the elevated walkway that led down to the lower docks where the boats were moored, crab traps hanging off the sides. We'd watch kids taking sailing lessons and James would drop a line off the far side of the floating dock in what seemed to be more of a meditative practice than an actual attempt to catch anything. When we invariably left with no fish, he'd reason that he needed to come back when it was cloudy to better his chances.

We'd realize it was approaching the ice cream hour and scramble to make it in time, because the shop closed at 5:00 and it was the only show in town. We'd drive down the winding main street, the wind in our sunburnt faces. In Maine, I was a window down girl. No AC for me. Late afternoon was my favorite time of day, except for all the others. We drove in the dappled sunlight, down the tree-lined road to the ice cream shop, with the music turned up and my tanned, bare feet on the dashboard.

The kids would spill out of the truck and race ahead to get in line. You would think eating ice cream at that time of day would spoil our appetite for dinner, but we were always hungry and the island always fed us.

I'd always say I wasn't sure I was going to get an ice cream, and then I always did. Java Crunch was my favorite. Dark chocolate-covered espresso beans in creamy coffee ice cream. Bittersweet has always kind of been my thing. We'd sit at the picnic tables in front of the shop and flirt with Shugy, the spoiled reprobate of a pug who owned the owner of the one antique store on the island. Shugy would waddle over and grace us with his presence if we shared our cones. Once the ice cream was gone, though, we were of no use to him and he would unceremoniously turn his corkscrew-tailed backside to us and leave, which only served to make us love him more.

———

The island wouldn't have been the island without a lobster bake. James would haul a huge pot of water outside out to a propane heater in the circular drive. The last couple of years, we got our lobsters from a local who lived in a tiny blue house perched right on the beach. He had a recreational license and would give us the lobsters for free on one condition. He simply asked that we bring the shells back to him after we were done so his adorable wife could leave them out for her pet seagull, Snowflake, who liked to peck at whatever meat we'd missed.

I'd coerce the boys into shucking corn on the steps of the deck, and we'd feast out at the picnic table next to the barn by the uneven stone wall that edged the meadow. By the time the last claw had been cracked, the last ear of corn stripped, and the last bit of butter sopped up, the sun would be waning. There was a particular light to those sunsets–I've never seen it anywhere else. It always reminded me of the Robert Frost line, *"Nothing gold can stay."* I'd frantically try and record it with my camera, but that sort of fleeting magic never translates, does it? Maybe it's not meant to be captured. We can't hold on to what's not ours.

We'd sit in the rose-gold light, full and content. The kids would get their fourth wind and tear around the yard, whipping the dogs into a frenzy. The adults would sit around chatting, and eventually move inside to light the fire and do the dishes. There was a comforting sameness to each day, but it was never boring. I found myself frequently overcome with love and gratitude for the people around me, and for having been welcomed so completely.

When I braved the Memory app that first summer after James and I split, it showed me on that day, the previous year, I was at my favorite place on earth with people I loved. People I considered family. I scrolled through the pictures and posts from that trip. I knew what was going on at that time. I knew how hard things were. I knew the pictures weren't telling the whole story. It's so funny: people say photographs don't lie, but that has not been my experience. Anyone who's ever scrolled back in time through their own Instagram feed knows that photos lie all the time. At best, it's a carefully curated truth. In any case, the face smiling back at me looked happy despite the truths not told, because I was always happy on the island. And ignorance is bliss. I didn't know it would be the last time.

I would say I'd have been more grateful and savored it more if I'd known, but I honestly don't know if I could have. I was always fully present there. I was always soaking it up. I always loved it for exactly what it was. I never needed to amplify or modify it. The only thing I ever wanted to change was the day we left. I was never ready to say goodbye. I wanted everything else to stay exactly as it was, even when the change was needed.

I wrote this the second-to-last summer I was there:

"The barn is being repaired. They're putting up siding which looks great, but I already miss the flaking paint. James came in a little while ago carrying a huge cow bone to show me. The guys found it when they were clearing brush away from the side of the barn in order to re-roof and shingle it. A cool and vaguely creepy reminder that this place was not always a family home. At one point in its history, this place was the Island's poor farm. If you were destitute or homeless or crazy or, say, alcoholic, you could come here and live and work and maybe even recover a bit. Come to think of it, perhaps not all that much has changed.

I've been sitting here in the breezeway which is my favorite place to write in the whole world. I'm watching the mist rise up off the meadow as it does every morning.

The barn has been re-sided and re-roofed because there were some intense storms last year that did a lot of damage. I miss the old chipping paint. They had to cut back the lilac trees that were growing right up against it in order to do the work. I'm a little heartbroken about that. Change is not my favorite unless it is my idea.

The storms that ravaged the island took out an unbelievable number of trees. Huge evergreens downed, with their entire root structures lifted up. Maybe because the soil is so rocky their roots spread wide rather than deep. The island looks different in some places now.

I resist change, whether it's a repainted barn, a pruned lilac, a felled tree, a child off to college, losing a pet, relationships that are still fractured. I want things to be what they were. I want things I love frozen in time, but the world simply does not work that way.

So, the barn is good for another hundred years. The lilac bushes will likely grow back healthier and more beautiful. There are new vistas on the island, space for new things to grow, openings through which you can now see the ocean."

I tried to remember the last meal I cooked there, the last sunset, the last ice cream cone, the last time I jumped off the dock. I wanted to frantically gather up all the memories and commit them to paper, so I wouldn't lose them. Those stories are like the mercury in an old-fashioned thermometer. Glistening, slippery, and a little toxic.

One morning on that last visit I wrote:

"It's 6:47 in the morning and I am sitting on a dock.

We went to bed early last night—we tend to do that in Maine. I finished my book and was asleep by 9:30. Woke up at 11:51 completely riddled with anxiety and grief. I'm not even entirely sure what I'm mourning. Strange. I usually sleep so well here.

There's no TV, so the usual Law & Order or HGTV fixes were not to be had. I went downstairs to the breezeway and listened to a couple of podcasts until my head and heart settled down and I could fall back asleep.

James came down early and said he wanted to fish while it was still cloudy—we're still pretending that's a thing, I guess. He wanted me to try and go back to sleep, but I knew the salty air, the gulls' cries, and the fog on the water would give me what I needed. This place comforts me in ways I can't explain.

I don't know why healing can't be linear and grief can't be efficient, I only know they're not.

We drove the short stretch of road to the water and walked past the boats and the empty crab pots to the end of the dock. James cast a line while I set up a chair. I'm drinking my coffee and shivering a little. It's a new day and the fish are jumping. There's a school of them off to the right and I can see their little fins cutting through the surface of the water. I comment that they look like tiny sharks. James says, 'You say that every time.'

He's right. I do. I say it every time."

On our second-to-last day, we headed out for one final hike. I remember the smell: soil, salt, and pine. If I could only smell one thing for the rest of my life it would be that combination. James parked on the shoulder of the road near the trailhead. Oddly enough, this was a trail we'd not explored before. We were filled with wonder that the tiny island could still have new gifts to offer even after all this time. We left the baking sun behind and eased into the marginally cooler woods. The boys bickered good naturedly, which allowed me to be quiet. I always felt less pressure to fill the silence there. Littlest shouted out in delight when he came upon a stretch of the trail covered in the smallest toads I'd ever seen. We hiked down by an inlet and marveled at the deer mounds in the tall grass at the water's edge. It was so beautiful. All of it. Even us. We were beautiful there. Even when things were hard. Somehow, we always seemed to be slightly better versions of ourselves on the island.

I appreciated it in the moment, but would I have been undone at its beauty if I'd known I wouldn't walk that trail again? Would it have been more beautiful? Could it have been? Or would the pain of knowing have taken me out at the knees? Or both?

Did he know it was my last time there? And why does knowing that feel important?

———

My last morning on the island, I rose early and wrote this:

"It's 5:39 in the morning and it's foggy out. It's chilly, so I put a sweater on over my pajamas and I'm shivering under a blanket waiting for the coffee to brew. Making coffee before you've had coffee is nearly impossible, but I'm doing it. People are using the word hero.

It's our last day. We'll drag our feet as much as possible, playing chicken with the last ferry. How late can we leave the farm and still be to the dock on time? We're already talking about squeezing in another weekend, maybe in the fall. And by we, I mean I. The island is stunning in autumn and I haven't had my fill of it this year.

I'm filled with gratitude for lots of reasons this morning. Sometimes the practice of gratitude is just noticing your life. Sometimes it's just taking in wonder and sharing it with someone. Marveling at the tiny toads carpeting a trail or counting the deer in a field at dawn. Savoring a lobster feast or playing a rowdy game of cards or sitting on the dock with the afternoon sun warming your face after plunging into icy water.

Sometimes the practice of gratitude is just showing up for your life wholeheartedly, being present and delighting in it. Isn't that what love is? Noticing? It's really just noticing, in the end.

What didn't I notice, though? What did I miss? There's a wistfulness in what I wrote, which I attributed to leaving. James always joked that I had a tantrum when it was time to depart, but maybe it ran deeper. Maybe the gentle admonishment to pay attention was meant for me. Maybe some part of me already knew.

Maybe I was already homesick.

The last morning, I looked over at the tree by the clothesline. It was strange not to see Diego, lolling underneath while we packed the truck for the return trip.

———

Diego was a flat-coated retriever with long, wavy, black fur, an elegant snout, beautiful brown eyes, and a flashy tail. He was our family pet, adopted when my kids were young and our family still lived in Seattle. He was the antithesis of Bad Dog. If the little Baddie was an alpha, Diego was the omega. Sweet and gentle and perfect. The farm in Maine was his favorite place, too. Sixty acres, no fences. We were all together every day, which was really the only thing he ever wanted, anyway. Fields to romp in. No leashes. Lots of obliging kids abandoning half-eaten food for him to steal. He was tennis ball obsessed–he once fit four in his mouth at the same time, an impressive, if slightly less-than-marketable skill–and he would chase them for as long as we would throw them.

I knew when it was time to let Diego go. It was probably past time, to be honest. I woke in the middle of the night to his cries and I knew. I stayed up the rest of the night with him, both because I could not sleep and because I couldn't un-know the truth that I would be saying goodbye to him. James drove me to the vet's office and helped me carry him in, because he could no longer walk. I tried to give the young man at the desk my name, but I burst out crying instead. His eyes filled with tears and he nodded.

He brought us to a private room. He asked me if he could hug me. I let him.

The vet who came in was incredibly kind. She told me to take my time. They had Hoodsie cups in a little freezer in the room. I gave him two. Why not? I held the icy cups in my hand as he half-heartedly licked them clean. He finally had chocolate. Bucket list item, checked.

When it came time to say goodbye, James said he couldn't handle it, and left to go sit in the car. I couldn't handle it either, but I stayed. Love stays. The vet gave Diego the first shot. Then the second.

Then the vet left.

It was just me and Diego.

Then, it was just me.

He always smelled so good. I thought back to when he was a puppy. We had sage growing wild in our backyard. I said back then that a dog could never smell better than he did after rolling around in it, but I was wrong. Every day of his life he smelled like sunshine and grass, except for his paws, which always inexplicably smelled like popcorn. I curled my body around his and we spooned on the cold, tile floor, with the jittery, fluorescent lights buzzing overhead. I buried my face in the silky fur of his neck. I couldn't believe I wouldn't ever hold him again. I inhaled deeply as though I could archive the memory of him in my lungs.

It took me a long time to pick up his ashes. Actually, I made James do it. I couldn't walk back into that place. They sat in his home office closet because I could not bear to look at the little purple bag that somehow, impossibly, contained the dog who was such an enormous presence in my life.

Diego's favorite spot at the farm in Maine was under the tree at the top of the driveway, next to the clothesline. That shady patch of grass was where he always retreated when the boys had worn him out throwing the tennis ball. We'd need to take it away to save him from himself, because he never voluntarily stopped a game of fetch. Once he surrendered, he'd lope over to that spot, and collapse in the shade, his dirty tongue a mile long.

I was so certain that was what heaven looked like for him. His actual field of dreams. My plan was to bury him under that tree, but in all the chaos of getting the truck packed for that last trip, I forgot to get the ashes out of the closet. I think I forgot, anyway. When we crested the hill coming up to the house and I saw the tree, I realized I didn't have them. I said to James, *"I can't believe I forgot them. Maybe we can come back in the autumn and I can do it then."* James didn't say anything.

Sometimes I mourn the fact that I didn't get to bury Diego where he was happiest, but maybe the universe conspired to keep me from leaving him somewhere I could never visit him. I still don't have a place for him to finally rest, no special place we've a connection to, so he's still in the purple bag–just in a different closet. I wonder how many closets 'til we're home.

I have a photo of me at the lighthouse near the ferry dock on the island, taken right before we left. I'm tanned and smiling. And so certain I'll be back. The kids and Bad Dog were expelling some last-minute energy before the six-hour ride to Connecticut. The truck always had far more space on the trip back. We always used up everything we brought. It's funny how much time and energy and patience it takes to reach an island, and then departing, you have less than you came with. Perhaps that's the nature of living on an island. In order to get what you need to survive, it almost always means leaving.

I genuinely thought it was the place I'd end up. I have a friend who always reminds me that feelings aren't facts. Well, they may not be facts, but that doesn't mean they're fiction. There's a specific grief when the thing you've lost still exists in the world. Not lost, but lost to you. It can somehow cause you to wish you didn't know it was an option. If I'd known I would lose it, would I have gone anyway? Would I have accepted the beauty if I could have foreseen the wreckage? Would I have let myself love it all so deeply if I had known what the cost would be?

Grief is funny like that. It causes you to look back on experiences like a detective, looking for clues of knowing; or like an appraiser looking to assign them value. It blurs the edges of some memories and calls others into sharp relief. It changes the light in your memories. Makes it more golden.

The grief just *was*. It did not need to be fixed or cheered up. This grief didn't need platitudes, or to be told home is "*something you carry in your heart.*" God. Even if it's true, those are the words of someone who has a home. Our spiritual and emotional lives are very often tethered to physical places. Our connection to those places can be divine and profound, and grief over the loss of them cannot be ameliorated by a cross-stitched slogan or meme.

Maybe like the trees on the island, the rocky foundation of my childhood meant my roots ran wide and not deep. Perhaps that was why I seemed to be perpetually uprooted. Not untethered, exactly, but not secure, either, and subject to violent disruption when life's storms rage through. The island was as close to a home as I'd ever come. A woman I know in recovery told me about a beach house she once had and lost as a result of her addiction. She said, "*I mourned it for so long, but now I think… some people never get that. I had that place for ten years. How lucky am I? It was a blessing.*"

I was blessed to have had beautiful experiences in this place I loved. This grief was simply the flip side of that. I wasn't sure I'd ever come to terms with the fact that my summers at the farm were over, but no matter how much pain I felt, I couldn't regret loving the island enough to be undone by the loss of it.

Chapter Eleven
Places

I first heard of the Wild Goose Festival in 2013. The headline speaker that year was Glennon Doyle, who I loved, and the musical act was the Indigo Girls. It was a pretty irresistible combination for me, and I became intrigued. Wild Goose is a communal celebration of spirituality, social justice, music, and art that takes place in the mountains of North Carolina every July. I guess it's considered Christian, but, like, table-flipping Jesus, Christian. And table-flipping Jesus is my favorite Jesus.

In 2016, my friend KB, told me I needed to apply to be a co-creator at the festival. I figured it was good practice in moving outside my comfort zone. I felt safe in doing it, though, because I was certain I'd never be chosen. I was barely sober a year, and trying to figure out what my life was supposed to be. I submitted a proposal to speak about the power of story, and how the way we tell our stories of harm can inform what we come to believe about them. As I read up more on the festival I became convinced that I wanted to attend, no matter what. When I was accepted as a co-creator I was terrified and thrilled in equal measure.

James and I flew into Asheville and rented a car. We drove forty-five minutes to Hot Springs through the impossibly green foothills of the Blue Ridge Mountains, dotted with dilapidated barns, tiny churches, and meadows. It was so beautiful that the violence of the all-too-frequent Confederate flags felt even uglier.

Reading through the extensive program that night, I noticed that every evening there was an event called "Beer and Hymns." That sounded... awesome. Love beer, love hymns. However, given that I'd recently celebrated a year of sobriety, I was a little nervous at precisely how great that sounded. I kept thinking about it, feeling preemptively left out of the experience–and as anyone in recovery knows, self-pity is dangerous territory.

The first morning there, I woke up in our tent. We were "glamping," except, no. We most certainly were not. The tent may have had electricity, but it bore no resemblance to the decked out boho extravaganza in the picture when we booked it. For the record? Twinkle lights, not included.

James was still sleeping when I got up and decided to hunt for coffee. As I walked down the dirt path toward the main stage where the food trucks were, I thought again about Beer and Hymns. What hymns, I wondered. And what beer? I was jolted out of my reverie by the sound of someone reciting the serenity prayer. I looked around and noticed a tent with a handful of people in a circle of folding chairs. I wandered in, sat down, and found myself at a recovery meeting. I could feel my shoulders lower and relax. It was the kind of tension you only notice once it releases. I felt instantly safer, just knowing the circle existed.

That night, after a long day of listening and dancing, praying and singing, hugging and reflecting, James and I went back to our tent to sleep. We were in bed, and the most amazing music began to swell around us. Even though I couldn't make out the words, I had a lump in my throat and my eyes began to tear up in the dark.

James whispered to me, "*I feel like we're missing out on something.*" We got up, threw on sneakers and stumbled to the Cafe tent. The band was The Many, and the woman singing had one of those voices with a built-in ache that just cracks me wide open. The song was *Lovely, Needy People*. The event was A Wild and Holy Late Night Communion. It was part liturgy, part performance art. It was a lament. I sat there, with tears streaming down my face. What was this place? The whole thing felt purposeful. I knew I was not there by accident.

"Oh you prisoners in your cells
All you in private hells
Kyrie eleison
All you hungry and ignored
Who thirst for something more
Kyrie eleison
You who feel so lost but are afraid of being found
You who are in chains but are afraid to live unbound
Kyrie eleison, kyrie eleison"

I sat there, with tears streaming down my face. The song tapped into a deep vein of loss I'd been unwilling to look at. Early recovery involves a ton of grief, and we probably don't talk enough about it. There's the loss of your coping mechanism, sure, but you're also grieving what you either lost or threw away as a result of your addiction; you're losing an identity–even if it's a negative one–and grieving relationships that have to change or end. Sobriety requires complete transformation, because otherwise what is the point?

I was in those mountains to float in a river and hang out with God. I was there to sit in on talks of race and gender, justice and forgiveness–and listen. I was there to spend important time with James and quietly walk through the woods with him. I was there to stop what I was doing every time someone wanted to tell me their story and I was there to bear witness. I was there to hug KB, a friend I'd only ever known online and on the phone, and I was there to push her gorgeous littles on swings and revel in their nonsense. I was there to dance sober under the stars.

And, as it turns out, I was in those mountains to grieve.

Wild Goose was, perhaps, the first place I'd ever been where people seemingly walked around with their insides on the outside. People seemed to be wide open, and comfortable with vulnerability and telling and hearing hard truths. Something about the level of honesty there felt like one big recovery meeting to me, Beer and Hymns aside. There seemed to be a general sense that it was not only okay to 'come as you are,' but an expectation that you do so.

The first recovery meeting I ever attended back in Connecticut was unbearable to me. It felt over-the-top positive and happy-clappy. I was crushingly hung over and in deep despair–and when you are in that place, hope and joy don't feel like an invitation, they feel like a con. At the second meeting I ever went to, though, a woman raised her hand to share and talked about her broken heart, her fears, and her mistakes. No one tried to fix her. No one tried to cheer her up. They just accepted her exactly where she was at and bore witness to her pain. It felt like what I imagine those places where they pipe pure oxygen into the room must be like–for the first time in my life I was really breathing. I felt suddenly and intensely *awake*. I was not at all sure I wanted to stop drinking, and I was almost positive I couldn't, but I wanted whatever was happening in that circle of women. Whatever it was, it felt like what I imagined home to be–but not any home I'd ever known.

Goose struck me the same way. I wasn't sure what exactly the hell was going on in those woods, but in a strange place with thousands of people I'd never met, I felt like I'd come home.

The next year I applied again, and was again accepted as a co-creator. James and I drove down that time, and took the boys. Again, I met amazing people, heard their stories, danced in the rain, and sat in that river. It all, every minute of it, felt like church.

The next two years I attended, James did not come with me. The first time it was his decision. The next time it was mine. As sad as I was that he wasn't there, it changed my experience in some profound ways. I drove down to North Carolina with one of my best friends, Johnny Sunshine. That's not his ACTUAL last name, though it should be. Fourteen hours in the car, forty-seven of them in Virginia. We decided there needed to be a new bumper sticker, *"Virginia is For Ever."* We never turned on the radio. We talked and talked and talked. And laughed. God, Johnny makes me laugh.

Matt and I were speaking together that year, so he was going to be there as well. I knew he and Johnny would love each other and I could not wait to get there, introduce them, and be back in those mountains.

One of the headline speakers that year was Barbara Brown Taylor. My friend Jessica loves her and references her often. Honestly, that should have been enough for me to go out and read everything BBT had ever written, but for whatever reason, I hadn't. Over the years, some of the speakers at Goose, like Reverend Otis Moss III and Dr. William Barber, thundered and rolled. Some speakers, like Jen Hatmaker, Jacqui Lewis, Mike McHargue, and Nadia Bolz Weber, made me laugh and cry. And some, like Barbara Brown Taylor, made me think.

She spoke of "thin places." There is a belief in ancient Celtic mysticism that thin places give us an opening into the Divine. That heaven and earth are only ever three feet apart, but in thin places, they're even closer. A thin place is where the veil between heaven and earth is lifted and we are more easily able to get a glimpse of God. She said she believes Goose is a thin place. I absolutely believe that to be true.

At Wild Goose, I walked around wide open. I smiled at strangers more, I initiated conversations more, and they went deep right away. There was precious little small talk at Goose. I found I was less quick to decide who people are before they had a chance to tell me.

I attracted stories like mosquitoes at Goose. They sought me out. I felt more at home in those woods surrounded by strangers and misfits, and in the little tent cul-de-sac we created on the banks of the French Broad River, than I did in neighborhoods where I lived for years.

The previous year, I'd agreed to lead one of the recovery meetings at the festival. I went into the tent when it was time, and there was one dude and me. He introduced himself; his name was Joe. I felt a little anxious because men sometimes make me anxious. He looked tough and kind of scary. He was covered in tattoos and shared openly about having been in prison. On the surface, he was very different from me, but the thing about Goose is that nothing ever stays surface-y there for long. I fidgeted and made awkward small talk until it became clear no one else was going to show up. We sat down and began to talk, and he started to tell my story. I mean, it was his, but aside from some details, like incarceration, it was mine. And when we got to talking about our addiction, the time in jail didn't seem all that different from me locking myself away in my bedroom to drink. There're all kinds of bars.

We were the same, Joe and I. We were exactly the same.

For the rest of the weekend, every time we saw each other we hugged. Joe came to my session to hear me speak and sought me out afterward to tell me what it meant to him and how he related to my talk on shame and trauma. We danced in the rain to the Red Dirt Boys. We were connected. I saw him near the food trucks right before we left and ran to him for one last hug. He said, *"Be good, darlin'."* I shouted back, laughing, *"You first!"* We talked about seeing each other the following summer–this man who initially made me so nervous, and who I might not have taken the time to get to know in another setting.

Is that because God is closer to me at Goose? I don't know. I wonder if it isn't less about the thinness between me and the Divine and more about my ability to be still and notice it. There's a saying in recovery that if you find yourself far away from God, you're the one who moved. I like the idea behind that even though I find the underlying premise to be utterly untrue.

The reality is I have never, ever been far from God. Not when I was furious, not when I said I didn't believe, never. Not when I was being abused as a child, not when I was an angry teenager, not when I was a terrified young, single mother, and not when I was a hopeless alcoholic. God was always with me, on the linoleum floor, in the college bar, in the rocking chair with my son at 3:00 a.m., and at rock bottom. Always. No more than three feet away. Sort of like a friendly version of the creature in *Alien*. You know that scene when Sigourney Weaver is staring straight ahead and the monster's face is right up against hers, off to the side?

In those moments I may have felt forsaken, but all I had to do was turn my head. Maybe thin places for me are the ones in which I have an easier time pivoting toward God. The spiritual teacher Ram Dass says, *"We're all just walking each other home."* That's the most accurate description of God I've ever heard.

I had so many moments up in the mountains of North Carolina when it was clear to me I was on holy ground. That something important was happening. Something sacred. That I needed to pay attention and be still–that I was called to bear witness.

When Johnny and I got there, we met up with Matt. My friend Cori, an Episcopal priest who I'd met and fallen in love with the previous year, was there too. We were all in the same little spot. Cori is the kind of camper that has a welcome mat outside her tent and a Dustbuster inside. She brings home with her, wherever she goes. I love her so much. We'd all requested campsites next to each other, and we arrived at Goose to find a happy little neighborhood of tents along the riverbank, just waiting for us to move in.

As we unloaded, we noticed a young woman trying to set up her single-person tent. She was the only person we didn't know in our cozy tent village, and she was sobbing. Johnny Sunshine immediately sat at the picnic table with her and started being Johnny Sunshine, so naturally, she told him all of the things. She told him the reason she was crying–I mean, other than the fact that setting up a tent by yourself is impossible–was that she'd planned on coming to Goose with her friend, a guy she met in recovery. He'd come the previous year, had a great experience and had talked her into accompanying her this year.

He'd died recently.

She'd come by herself in the hopes of meeting someone, anyone, who knew him, which was admittedly a long shot at a festival of 4,000 people.

I walked over to the picnic table and Johnny told me a bit of her story; she was still crying. She asked me if, by chance, I'd met him. She pulled up a photo on her phone and handed it to me. I looked down at the picture and realized I was in a sacred moment.

I sat still on the bench with the sound of the river rushing behind us, with three feet of picnic table between us, and talked to her about her friend. My friend.

Joe.

I didn't need to turn my head to know that the face of God was right beside me.

There came a time in the year 2020 when it became apparent that Wild Goose would not be taking place. When we first went into lockdown they were saying there was still a chance it would happen, but eventually, the reality settled in. It would not be possible for that band of holy mischief-makers to converge on the river running through those verdant mountains.

I am not being overly dramatic when I say I was devastated. If there was ever a year my soul needed the balm of Goose, it was that one. It was the last place that felt like home that I could still access. I always looked forward to heading to those hills and that river, but in 2020, in the aftermath of my life being turned upside down, the pull felt urgent. I felt disconnected, as though I could fly off into space at any moment. I needed to sit in the shallow, rushing river. I needed to tilt my chin up and feel the sun on my face. I needed to meditate with dragonflies zipping around me and music filtering through the trees. I needed to dance in the rain, pray unabashedly, and sit around the fire and talk about things that mattered.

For the first summer in a very long time, the two places I felt most at home in the world were not available to me. Summers had long been about the island and those mountains, and now the circumstances of the breakup and the shutdown prevented me from going home to them when I needed them most.

In the weeks leading up to when Goose would have been held, I spent so much time thinking about what should have been taking place. As a person in recovery, I knew I must try to accept things as they were, but the Wednesday of that week I couldn't help but feel I *should* be in the car with Johnny Sunshine talking and laughing and driving to one of my thin places.

Wild Goose, like the island, was a place where I didn't time travel. I didn't need to. Those two places slowed me down. I even walked slower. I am a super-fast walker by nature. I strolled at Goose. I meandered. I could sit still and do nothing. I wasn't on to the next thing in my head. I was not mentally multitasking. What that meant was that I fully experienced everything and everyone both places had to offer—and perhaps that just meant I was *aware* that God was right here, in the messy middle of things with me.

Over the years, Wild Goose served as a midwife to my evolving and strengthening faith. It was a place that encouraged me to tell my stories and a place where I attracted the stories of others. It was a place where I came home to myself. It was a place where I felt wholly loved and seen. Even though I was only there for a handful of days every year, in the filtered sunlight of those woods I seemed to put down roots even as I was stretched up and out, just beyond where my comfort ended. Goose has always accepted me for exactly who I am and then always, always challenged me to grow.

Sitting in that fast, shallow river, hanging on to a rock, and chatting with friends and God feels more like church to me than any polished pew I've ever sat in. As I walked around Goose I could feel God nudging me to remember: *This* is who you are. Come home to yourself. Stay open. Listen. Feel. Eat. Dance. Pray. Laugh. Love.

When someone asks me where I'm from, it's a little hard to answer without giving my geographical resume. I grew up in Massachusetts, and while I still have family there, I have no home to go back to. I lived in Seattle for eleven years, but there's too much painful history there. When I go back to visit I feel like I'm crawling out of my skin. I've lived in Connecticut for seven years, and while I've come to feel comfortable here, it still feels temporary in some ways. It's not part of my identity. I always feel like either a visitor or a trespasser. There was no place I could go back to and exhale. No matter how hard I tried, I couldn't seem to find and keep a place where I felt safe and connected and known, and the places where I did feel those things didn't belong to me.

I moved to New Haven just before the pandemic, I was uprooted from my recovery community, most of my family lived far away, and my two favorite places—my spiritual homes—were lost to me, one for that year, one forever. I had incredible people in my life. I had real connection and love. I had community and a work family I treasured, but I didn't have a home. I didn't have that touchstone. And I thought, you know? Maybe I don't get that. We don't all get everything. Maybe there was no place like that for me. No place like home.

Chapter Twelve
Foundations

The house I grew up in was a little white ranch, perched at the top of one hill and the bottom of two others: the mid-point in a Y of streets in a blue collar neighborhood in a suburb just south of Boston. I was in first grade when we moved there; my parents, my two sisters, and me. There were three bedrooms, though my older sister's was little more than a walk-in closet. Still, it was her own, which felt fancy. My younger sister and I shared a room. We couldn't agree on a color so my mother found checkered bedspreads that had both her pink and my turquoise, and we transformed our bunk beds into a jungle gym, a ship, a rocket, or a castle, depending on the day.

We lived near the center of town, what we called The Landing, and up the hill from the big Catholic church where I received my first communion and the parochial school next to it, where I later broke up with God. A sweet elderly couple lived on one side of us, a big unruly Irish family on the other.

I suppose it was probably cute enough when we moved in, though I don't remember. In any case, years of poverty and neglect took care of that. Our house was *that* house. The one the neighbors talked about. The eyesore. The house with the peeling paint, sagging retaining wall, broken garage door window, and a lawn that always seemed to be waist high. Every now and then we'd come home and in our absence, someone would have cut it. More than likely one of our neighbors mowed it, which may well have been an act of kindness. It felt like judgment, though, because shame is a terrible translator.

In the backyard, there was a huge hole for a pool that never went in, dug before my parents divorced. It's curious to think there were plans to do something like that even as our family was unraveling. I get it, though. Seems sort of aspirational, like maybe that's the kind of family we all hoped we'd be. My dad left and nothing was ever done with it. It just stayed there, a gaping dirt hole of good intentions.

It's funny how just about anything can become normalized. We were imaginative little girls who could always find a way to incorporate whatever circumstance we were dealt into our play life. No lights? We were the Ingalls girls surviving the long winter. Cold house? We slid around the wood floors in our socks pretending to be ice skating.

Giant hole in the middle of our backyard? The perfect stage for us to put on a show.

Eventually the disappointment over what it was supposed to be gave way to acceptance of what it was: a massive gouge inflicted on the grassy slope of our backyard which, over time, filled up with weeds, like a wound left to heal in whatever way it could.

That tiny house was a house of scarcity. We lived in New England and frequently endured frigid winters with no oil for heat, no electricity, and, occasionally, no running water. During those times, we relied on kerosene lamps and yahrzeit candles in the evenings. The lamps were good because they were brighter, but we used the candles more because they were inexpensive and weirdly always available. Yahrzeit candles are traditionally used by Jewish families in mourning. We may have single-handedly created a market for them in our almost exclusively Irish and Italian town. Three little sort-of Catholic girls doing our homework by the light of grief.

When it got bitterly cold, all of us slept in the living room huddled together for warmth. Our clothes were dirty more often than not, and because showers with cold water are a tough sell, so were we.

Ours was not a house with a full fridge, or even a working fridge for that matter. I remember doing the math that one of my best friends, Ellen, was rich because there were leftovers in her refrigerator regularly. Not only was there food, there was so much they couldn't finish it. It blew my mind. Looking back, they weren't rich. They just weren't poor.

Our house was not a house where you freely invited friends over, or even answered the door when someone came to it unexpectedly. An unanticipated knock would induce panic, and a wild-animal stillness would come over us. We'd silently freeze until the knocking stopped and whoever it was gave up and went away. I can't remember ever calmly answering the door; it simply wasn't something we did. That's just not how shame works.

When I'd been married twelve years, we moved into what was supposed to be our dream home just before my fortieth birthday. For the first time in my life, I felt some semblance of financial security. We'd lived modestly for a long time, my husband had become quite successful, and we finally sold our starter home. The new house was an enormous Cape, nestled on a beautiful lot that was just shy of an acre. There was a multi-level deck out back, and a gazebo in the yard. My best friend Angela lived just on the other side of a little greenbelt; I could walk to her backyard by way of a pretty little path through the woods. I'd had my eye on the property for years, and when it finally made its way onto the market and we were in a position to buy it, I was overjoyed. I wandered around it frequently in those early days thinking, *I cannot believe this is my life.**

About a month after we moved in, my then-husband was in his office, just off the sunlit foyer. The wood floors in the entryway led to a grand staircase, and double doors opened out to a porch that spanned the front of the house. It was pristine, not a thing out of place. Ever. I was standing in the hall just outside his office talking to him, and the doorbell rang unexpectedly. He must have seen my reaction. A look of mild exasperation came across his face. "*Just answer it*," he said.

That's so completely reasonable. I knew that even as I stood there frozen and sweating, trying to will myself to move toward the door. You know, like a normal person.

Less than two years later, I'd stand in the driveway selling my things in a moving sale because my marriage had imploded and the house was on the market. Women with whom I'd served on PTA committees rifled through the lovely things I'd collected to make the house feel like home, looking for bargains. I was watching the life I'd worked so hard to build be sold off for parts. The shame was overwhelming. When I think back, I remember how foolish I felt. Initially I thought, *"I cannot believe this is my life."* But as the shock wore off it turned into *"Of course. Of course this happened. This was always going to happen. You're so stupid. You let your guard down. You never deserved this."*

The thing about formative years filled with scarcity, chaos, and shame is that want and fear get embedded into your very bones. You can work against it. You can know it's there and do all the things to address it. You can surround yourself with abundance and order and light. That's all well and good–but even so, every now and then your bell will get rung.

That's just how trauma works. Not memories so much as time travel. Something triggers you and you go hurtling back to when it was cold and dark and hard.

It was cold and dark and hard a lot of the time.

My mother, my sisters, and I moved out of that dingy little ranch when I was twenty-one. For me, there was no affection or melancholy in the departure. I didn't feel sentimental the way so many of my friends did when saying goodbye to their childhood home. I walked through the empty rooms, filled the last box, checked the dank cellar one final time, flew up the open staircase with my heart pounding the way it always did, and walked away. No wistful look in the rearview mirror.

Leaving was easy.

Some years ago, when I was visiting a friend who still lives in the town where I grew up, I went to see it. Just a drive-by. I was weirdly anxious about being recognized, as though I was doing something wrong just by being there. The people who bought it renovated it extensively. They even raised the roof. It was unrecognizable. Now it's a perfectly lovely 1800 square foot colonial, almost too big for the lot it's on. It's nestled on a manicured lawn with a bright turquoise front door, a crisp American flag, and a wooden stoop that bears no resemblance to the crumbling cement steps with the flaking paint we walked up to get to the front door that no one ever answered. All the other houses looked pretty much the same, though. It's the oddest thing—as though someone line-item vetoed our childhood. It's almost like it didn't happen, it's been cleaned up so well.

I went on one of those realtor websites recently and looked at the satellite view, and wouldn't you know it? There's a goddamned pool in the backyard.

You know when you bang your shin on something really hard but it doesn't leave a mark? There's almost a feeling of disappointment that there's no spectacular bruise to tell the story of what happened to you. When something hurts that much, it's insulting not to have something to show for it. We all want a little proof of harm because invisible injuries are somehow trickier to heal.

A while back, one of my sisters recounted a conversation she had with a lifelong friend who was reminiscing about candle-lit nights at our house and how much she had loved them. When you've endured something traumatic and someone not directly impacted recalls their experience of it, it can be difficult. Everything looks and feels different from the outside and I understand wanting to focus on the positive, but it can feel like an erasure. My sister said, *"That wasn't fun. Not for us. You know that, right?"*

The novelty of one cold, dark night caused by a storm-induced power outage is quite a different experience than a cold, dark night followed by an endless stream of cold, dark nights, with precious little hope of it ever changing.

There is a test called the ACES test; the acronym stands for Adverse Childhood Experiences. It's essentially a screening for childhood trauma. Not all of the questions on it relate to overt acts of harm, some of them pertain to more everyday things. Did you have enough to eat? Did you have clean clothes? Now, hunger and dirty clothing may not sound traumatic to you, per se, but a component of trauma is powerlessness, and as a child you have limited agency over if and how your basic needs are met.

When you dread silent study before lunch because your stomach is growling so loudly the kids around you are laughing, that's different than just being hungry. When you only have two outfits, worrying that they smell musty or that people will notice that the spot from something spilled on your shirt last week is still there, that's different than wearing the same sweater twice before laundering it.

One Christmas, when I was in high school, my mom got me an outfit for my gift. There were neon plaid pants, suspenders, an electric pink shirt, and matching tulle hair bow. Good Lord. It was the '80s and we were all doing our best. I absolutely loved it. I couldn't believe it was mine. Now, as a mom, I understand what it must have meant to my mother to give me something like that, a gift I was so excited about. It was trendy and I hadn't really ever had anything like that before. I was so proud of it. I could not wait to wear it to school.

There was this one girl, Tiffany. She was cool. She had short spiky hair, and a distinct style: baggy, pegged pants, shirts buttoned up to her neck, stacks of plastic bracelets. So preppy it was punk, if that makes sense. She looked hard. A smidge left of center, but not so out there that she didn't fit in. She was also a little mean, but funny–a combination that makes an incredibly effective weapon. She lived on the cusp of popularity, not really one of the golden ones, but not wildly unpopular, like me. She was in-crowd adjacent. The hierarchy of belonging in adolescence is vicious and universal. I think it's why *The Hunger Games* books were so popular. We all recognize the bloodsport.

Maybe Tiffany developed all those sharp edges in self-defense, perhaps to project an air of not caring. Who the hell knows what was going on in her home? I'm sure she had her own story to tell. We all do. I don't know. In any case, I wore my new outfit to school after the holiday. Then I wore it over, and over, and over. One day in Psychology class (you can't make this shit up) she said loudly, and in a voice dripping with all the chemical sweetness of diet soda, *"I really love that outfit, Laura. Why don't you wear it to school AGAIN?"*

I was humiliated. I spent the rest of the day drenched in shame. I went home, took the outfit off and swore I'd never wear it again. I did, obviously. I had to. But never with joy. And never all together—which may have actually been an act of the fashion gods. Perhaps Tiffany was an angel of some sort. It was a lotta look. Anyway, that's when I learned to buy neutral clothes with no print. If you have to wear something over and over again, make it forgettable. I have always been pretty good at finding ways to disappear. Today, I have an appalling amount of clothing. It's ridiculous. In the grand scheme of things, though, as a drug of choice, sweaters are fairly harmless. I still gravitate toward black and grey and white, but I force myself to buy clothing with color and pattern–and hand-to-God, every time I do, I think of Tiffany.

The first autumn we were together, Shane and I went to Vermont for the weekend. The place we stayed happens to be just down the way from the house where he grew up. I knew a little about his childhood, he knew a lot about mine. I tend to be pretty open. Plus, most of my stuff is out there in the world, so I generally own it all up front. He is slower to share. We were still in that stage of learning each other's histories. He's not a man who offers things up easily. Some people are open books, and some people share a chapter only every now and again, so when the stories come, they're a gift.

That Saturday, we drove down a winding, country road, the trees ablaze in a radiant patchwork of crimson and gold. Vermont is such a show off in the fall. We began dating just before the pandemic, and so in the absence of normal life most of our early dates were hikes and long, unplanned drives in the Connecticut countryside listening to music and talking. This sunny, idyllic autumn day was perfect for just such a drive, but it didn't feel as though we were meandering. There was no music and he was driving with purpose.

He pulled over to the side of the road and said, "*This is where we lived.*" We got out of the car and I looked around. A little way off in the distance there was a newer farm house nestled down in a little valley, complete with a tin roof and a tidy red barn. The stuff of postcards. It was so beautiful. He pointed to the woods on the other side of the farm and said, "*I used to hunt there.*"

"*You did?*"

"*Yes,*" he said. "*My dad would hand me the shotgun and tell me to go get dinner.*" He said, "*I'd get a squirrel or two, sometimes.*" He laughed the way you do at things that aren't funny. "*The shotgun was as big as I was.*"

I looked at his handsome profile. That feeling you get when you know something significant is happening washed over me. "*How old were you?*"

"*Eleven, maybe? Twelve?*"

I let the weight of that settle on my heart. I looked down at my boots in the drift of brilliantly colored leaves withering by the side of the dirt road. I breathed deeply in the crisp, cold air that carried the scent of a season where beauty is born of thousands upon thousands of lovely little deaths: a hint of wood smoke and sadness.

I closed my eyes and stood in the quiet for a minute, because that's what you do when you're on sacred ground. Suddenly, the radio being off made sense. There are moments in time for which the only appropriate soundtrack is silence.

"Where is your house?"

"It's right there." He pointed to a spot just beyond where we'd parked. It was a pile of rotten wood collapsed in on itself and a hole in the ground that was only identifiable as a dirt basement if you knew what you were looking for. He went on to tell me that at one point his dad poured some cement and he and his little brother made handprints in it. I tried to picture a smaller version of the strong, capable hands I'd grown to love pressing down into the cool, wet mixture.

I asked, *"Do you have good memories from here?"*

"No," he said, without looking at me.

He walked away from his sports car, so immaculate it could have come straight from the showroom floor, and hopped down into the hollowed ground. I was there but he was alone, the way we always are in those moments, in those holes. He walked the perimeter as best he could, meticulously lifting debris and peering underneath. I instinctively knew he was looking to see if he could find the concrete remnant among the rubble. I recognize emotional archeology when I see it. Anything can become treasure if it costs you enough.

When we picture people digging for antiquities, our minds automatically go to mummies and pyramids, but most of the time the sites are more mundane than that. Scientists sift through the dirt looking for material remains of what life was really like in a given place in a given era.

Over time, the actual structures of a civilization fall prey to age and elements, and we're left with holes in the ground, overgrown and filled with shards of a life that serve as evidence of how people survived. Or didn't. The foundations, the ruins, tell the story.

When foundations are unstable they profoundly impact

whatever is built on top of them. Shoddy materials, inexpert handiwork, or exposure to water, wind, heat and cold–even the relentless march of time can create fissures that undermine a structure's foundation. A compromised foundation ensures that anything built on top of it becomes unsafe. Living there isn't sustainable without a hell of a lot of repair work.

Same with human beings.

On the drive home to Connecticut, we were both pretty quiet. I have no idea what was going on in his head. I was rearranging puzzle pieces in mine. That's what stories do. They give us insight into what lies underneath the person we think we know–they provide the missing parts that, once in place, help the whole picture make sense.

Frequently in fiction, a writer will take their readers back in time to share information that provides context for how a character became who they became. They're called origin stories. A rich guy dressing up as a bat and running around Gotham fighting crime is interesting enough, I guess, but it becomes compelling when we learn that young Bruce Wayne witnessed his parents' murder and could do nothing to save them.

Most of my favorite people had the seeds of their art and purpose and passion planted in the dark, deep holes of their formative years. We call them that for a reason, I guess. The woman I am grew up out of that foundation. I remember the first time I heard Glennon Doyle talk about 'sistering,' the practice in building where you shore up a beam or a joist by bringing other beams alongside it to strengthen it enough to bear the weight it is carrying. When I heard that, I immediately thought of my two sisters, one older, one younger, on either side of me, all of us carrying such heavy things.

That little white house did the best it could given all the things, and so did *everyone* in it. I really do know that. There are aspects of my character and personality that are rooted in that foundation that I wouldn't change if I could. I get my work ethic and my generosity from my mother. Anything I know about resilience and loyalty, I learned from my sisters. There are also stories that were written inside those walls that impact me to this day. Stories of scarcity and danger, stories of want and need. I used to think growing up the way we did was a curse. Then I grew to believe that some of it was a blessing. Now I think it's neither. Or both. It simply was. Is.

Heather King wrote, *"I once heard a sober alcoholic say that drinking never made him happy, but it made him feel like he was going to be happy in about fifteen minutes."* That's sort of what home is like for me. I've lived my life feeling like home is right around the corner, just out of reach, once everything aligns and falls into place- as though it is something that can be arranged or achieved outside of oneself, when the reality is that I'm chasing the idea of safety and love and comfort–piling things and people up on an unsteady foundation, and calling it home.

Chapter Thirteen

Homecoming

A few years back, I was talking to a friend and she mentioned that she's been doing yoga. I said, *"Oh, I didn't know you practice yoga!"* Her reply knocked me back on my heels:

"I am finally making an amends to my body."

Oh.

Oh *shit.*

You know when you have one of those before and after moments? Like, there was a *before I heard that thing* and an *after I heard that thing*, and turns out, they're gonna have to be different. I have a love/hate relationship with those moments because they always require me to change.

For years, I had a serious lower back issue. It was debilitating and life impacting. I could not bring myself to see a doctor—which is a total trauma thing. It is one of the most common things I hear from fellow survivors. We will leave medical issues untended for so long that minor, treatable things become catastrophic. In particular, dental care and reproductive health. Anyway, it is something I have always done. No preventative measures; instead, powering through things that became more serious and painful than they needed to. *"I'll be fine. I can handle it."*

It makes perfect sense when you think about it. We take care of the things we value.

Accurately predicting that left to my own devices it would not be dealt with, James bought me a year's worth of massages as a Mother's Day gift. I frequently couldn't lie in one position long enough to complete the session and I wouldn't let them anywhere near my lower back. I would have the masseuse focus on my shoulders and neck, both of which were affected by the things I did to compensate for and work around my daily battle with pain. I was too afraid to tackle the actual problem, so I settled for managing symptoms.

It was recommended that I see a reflexologist, which I thought was a little woo-woo but did anyway. The practitioner asked me where my pain was. I told her and she said, *"Lower back pain is impacted by your first and second Chakras. They represent sex, money, and control."* She went on to explain that the chakra at the base of the spine is the root chakra, and it represents your foundational beliefs, values, and identity, and is closely tied to core issues such as survival and your relationship to money. The chakra located in the lower back and pelvis area is known as the sacral chakra, and has to do with early childhood, and relates to sexuality and your creative life.

Thank goodness I don't have issues in any of those areas. Close call.

I am a survivor of childhood sexual trauma, and my abuser was my paternal grandfather. While my abuse did not take place in the house where I lived, it took place in my family and home is more than the structure you live in. Home is the people in your life. Your family. That home, your family, is the one place where you should feel completely loved and totally safe. In *The Body Keeps the Score*, Bessel van der Kolk writes, *"Traumatized people chronically feel unsafe inside their bodies: The past is alive in the form of gnawing interior discomfort. "* The violent abuse I endured at my grandfather's hands was not just a violation of my body. It compromised the very idea of home for me. If you're not safe in your own body, you understand you are not safe anywhere.

The notion that this enduring pain I had was tied to that trauma was just unacceptable to me. I had done so much work to heal. I was thoroughly pissed off that my abuser was still impacting my daily life, more than three decades later. Dead and *still* causing me pain. I wanted it to be about something else. *Anything* else. I wanted this to be a purely physical problem. *I* wanted to decide what it was about. I wanted it to be solved *medically.*

I said something to her about how several members of my immediate family had undergone back surgery and that I knew I would eventually have to do the same but I wanted to forestall it. She then said, *"You know, you can choose to heal differently. "*

I stuck with reflexology for a while and it helped. It gave me some relief from what had become unmanageable pain. Eventually, I found a massage therapist who was very intuitive and that made an enormous difference. Going to the same person week after week rather than just booking whoever was available was important. She got to know me, know my body–probably better than I did in some ways. She said things to me like, *"You know what to do with pain."* *"You carry a lot of pain in your body."* and *"You know, just because you can endure a certain level of pain doesn't mean you need to. "*

She's also the one who told me that my face doesn't register pain. That she can be doing something she knows must be painful and there will be no way to discern from my expression that anything is happening. I'm embarrassed to admit it, but I always kind of considered my ability to endure and ignore pain stoically a superpower. It never occurred to me that pain is a message. Sometimes an alarm, sometimes a nudge–but always an indicator. Always an invitation to notice.

My unwillingness to acknowledge and attend to my pain goes beyond the physical. My massage therapist's gentle admonishment seemed so obvious when she said it. Just because a level of pain is survivable doesn't mean it's mandatory. How much harm had I done to my body and my spirit by soldiering on when surrender was an option? How often had I opted for fear and loneliness because I knew I could live through it? Like so many things that end up being destructive, it started off as a coping mechanism. My dogged determination to trudge on despite the pain I was in is, in no small part, why I'm here today. It's why I survived. It was a tool when I had no other resources or options, and weapons that start off as tools are the hardest to pry from our fingers. No matter how damaging they've become, we can't believe we cannot get them to work for us again. It was true for me when I was starving myself. It was true for me when I drank. And it was true for me in relationships.

I heard what my friend said about making an amends to her body and I couldn't unhear it. It just kept following me around, nipping at my heels. I knew I needed to do the same, even though I didn't know where to begin. The truth is so stupidly insistent. In sobriety, at least in my recovery community, we talk a lot about amends. What does and what does not constitute a real amends. An amends is not simply saying you're sorry and it's not about being forgiven. That may or may not happen as a result, but if it does, it's ancillary. It's about owning your behavior, and making things right if you can. There are all different ways it can be done, and not everyone will allow you to do it the way you might want. Ultimately, a necessary component of a proper amends is change. A willingness to live differently.

Making an amends can be daunting. Sometimes you have to work up your courage. Some are done quickly, some take years. I was also taught that you cannot make an amends until you have worked through any and all resentment toward the person/place/institution to whom you are making it. Until you've done that work you cannot be in the right space. You will look to defend or justify, or *"but, YOU..."* and none of those things have any place in it. You go in unarmed. You go in peace.

No wonder it has taken me so long. I've waged war with my

body for my entire life.

I decided to pay attention to my body. I made a promise to look at the messages my body sent me not as demands to be ignored or judged but as invitations to be different. I committed to honoring what my body needed rather than punishing it for not doing what I wanted or being what it was. I vowed to remember that the answer to exhaustion is rest, not martyrdom and caffeine, and that hunger is neither an emergency nor a threat. I began to realize that when I spoke violence to and about my body, I became my own abuser, and that my body is more than what happened to me.

For a long time, my favorite part of Goose was the Wild and Holy Late-Night Communion–that same event that drew James and I out of our tent that first night, years ago. Lenora Rand is the beautiful writer behind much of the liturgy and lyrics that accompanied those experiences. There was a theme every year and one year it was about our bodies. She asked me to create something for the event. Pro-tip: if you fan-girl relentlessly, sometimes something great comes out of it. I was more than a little intimidated both because I don't really write poetry, but also because I had never spoken in public about my abuse. I'd written about it, and I'd spoken about the effect it had on me, but I hadn't ever stood in front of a crowd and told them what happened to me. All my public speaking had been from the vantage point of survival; I hadn't passed the mic to my eight-year-old self to tell her story from the inside.

I was incredibly nervous. Johnny and Matt both tried to calm me down, to no avail. I think Lenora could see how scared I was. I told her why and she said in the quietest, kindest of voices, *"Oh."* I don't know why that helped, but it did.

By the age of eight, I wanted to leave my body.

I hadn't even been there all that long when you think about it.

This body. God-given. Beloved, necessary, enough.

Built for me to inhabit. Frame of bone, walls of skin and flesh.

The only home I can't run away or be evicted from, and yet.

Before, I was a skinny girl. I ran and played and danced with abandon.

I was scrappy and fast and free. My body was just that. MINE.

But the world told me otherwise because men want closed borders,

except. when. they. don't.

Sit in Santa's lap. It doesn't matter if you're scared. You're crying and you're saying no and the adults are telling you to smile pretty.

So, I smiled pretty.

Give Grampa a kiss. It doesn't matter if you don't want to. It's not nice to say no, and little girls are supposed to be nice.

It will hurt his feelings if you say no. We can't have that.

So I kissed.

One day, Grampa takes me for a walk, which is special, right? He doesn't ask anyone else. I go with him to walk the dog—he knows I love dogs. We're walking through the black-eyed Susans, and then suddenly there is a big hand up my shirt, and then, down my shorts and he says,

"Let me feel your little body."

I think, "This is weird," but I don't tell because I'm an obedient girl, a nice girl, and I've learned that this body is not really mine anyway.

I've always been a quick study.

And then it happens again, and again.

My home, my body becomes a little less mine. It feels a little less safe.

I realize my home is a

dangerous neighborhood.

I learn how to be outside my body. It becomes a recurring problem because he

won't. stop. trespassing.

It stops being weird and starts being scary,

but I don't tell because I'm a good girl. A nice girl.

And anyway, how do you make someone leave property you don't own?

Then one day, I say NO to Grampa. I tell him to get off my property.

I'm not being very nice.

But he doesn't listen because he doesn't think I'm the homeowner.

So he storms in anyway. He takes whatever he wants.

There's a home invasion on the cold, linoleum floor.

I look at the bowl of wet cat food by my head,

hold my breath,

and try very hard not to die.

So what do you do when you wake up every morning inside your own crime scene?

Well, you don't spend much time there. You float away.

You starve it, you numb it, you exercise it to death.

You let people use it as a playground. Why not? It's public property.

You take showers so hot your skin is scalded, but you're never. quite. clean.

I spent most of my life trying to make it pretty, decorating it, downsizing it, putting up tidy white picket fences.

Trying to make it nice enough that no one would notice the yellow tape across the front door.

Coming home to God took decades.

Coming home to my body, this body. Built for me to live and love in by God.

Frame of bone, walls of skin and flesh.

Beloved. Necessary. Enough.

That's taking longer.

It took longer. It has taken my whole life. I was working on forgiving myself for all of the harm I had done to my body and accepting the invitation to live differently in it. Perhaps, in the end, my inability to have or hold onto a home had something to do with my unwillingness to *be* one.

Chapter Fourteen
Luggage

Our first summer together, Shane was intent on us getting away, despite the pandemic. I had never been in an adult relationship where there were no kids to consider, so the pull to get away on a grown-up vacation was not as strong for me. I'd been a mom for twenty-eight years, and had spent the last seven with two boys who had camps and activities to manage all summer long. All my vacations were family-centered, so the notion of planning a vacation for just the two of us was a little alien to me.

At the time, Shane's son lived in Oregon and mine lived in Washington State. We decided to plan a trip to the Pacific Northwest so we could see both of them. We'd fly into Portland and drive to the beautiful, wild Oregon coast and then make our way inland to see his son first, then mine. It was our first real vacation together, and as we started to plan our trip some very real differences in the way we approached things began to make themselves known.

There's a saying, *'The way you do anything is the way you do everything.'* When it comes to Shane, nothing has ever been more true. I found myself in seemingly endless conversations about hotels.

At one point, I texted Matt to say, *"He's reading the car rental agreement. Aloud."* I finally told him I would rather forgo a car and walk the 242 miles from Cannon Beach to Bend than talk about the rental car for one more moment. He laughed at me, even though I wasn't joking, and agreed to handle it solo. The same was true for the hotel. I tend to not care all that much. If it's clean, I'm good. Matt and I talk a lot about the way our childhoods show up in this way. We're 'make-do' people and sometimes that leads to us settling for people, places, and situations that are less than ideal.

Shane is not that way. He is detail-oriented and methodical and cares about *everything*. The evening we arrived, when I texted Mary a photo of the view I had from the bed in our hotel room, overlooking Haystack Rock and the breathtakingly beautiful sunset, she replied that she was glad Shane chose the place, because she knew that as long as there wasn't a chalk outline on the floor, I'd have been okay with it. She wasn't wrong.

The next morning, we woke early and walked down the endless steps to the beach. It was chilly, and tendrils of fog still played in the sunlight. The gulls circled and complained, and Shane and I walked in silence on the cold, wet sand, patterned with undulating lines left by the receding tide. Haystack Rock, the enormous seastack many people know from the movie *Goonies*, loomed behind us, and brown pelicans swooped overhead. At one point, as we stood looking up at the cliffs, I went to take a photo of our shadows on the sand. It was hard to determine where I ended and he began. I backed away so there was daylight between us.

The following morning, we got into our totally perfect, thoroughly researched rental car and drove the five hours to Bend. For a long stretch of the trip, we were driving through the Cascade mountain range. The winding road was lined on either side by towering Ponderosa pine trees. The only station that came in on the radio was old-timey country. Reception wasn't great and the occasional wheezy sound lent an air of nostalgia that felt right. I was excited for the trip and nervous to meet his son. Not because I was afraid it wouldn't go well, but because I was sure it would.

I could feel the sharp hospital corners I was keeping on everything beginning to loosen. The delineation between my life and his life was starting to blur. It felt right, like the natural next step.

It also felt dangerous.

Bend is a high desert, surrounded by gorgeous mountains. The Deschute River runs through town, and we spent a fair amount of time in the Old Mill District with Shane's son, having meals, walking its banks, and talking. Bend is an outdoor-person's paradise, so during our stay there, we decided to head to Smith Rock for a hike. And by we, I mean, of course, Mr. Energy. Smith Rock is a magnet for rock climbers and hikers, and, apparently, us. It was a delightfully temperate 93 (freaking) degrees. When we arrived at the base and descended to the trail head, I saw the marker.

Misery Ridge.

"Shane. It's called Misery Ridge."

"Yes, sweetheart."

"Shane."

"C'mon! It'll be great!"

It was not great. It was UP. A *lot* of up. Steep, dusty, 93-degree, no shade, straight UP. Mr. Energy kept looking back, shouting, *"You're doing GREAT, SWEETHEART!" "Let's GOOOOOO."* Eventually, I pleaded with him to stop saying words, and he did. When we reached the summit, a sheer cliff overlooking the Crooked River, he stood victorious, surveying the view from 3,360 feet above sea level. I didn't have the heart to break it to him that everything the light touched was not his. I sat, drinking water and making snarky videos.

When we'd rested a bit—too long by his measure, not long enough by mine—he pulled me to my feet and kissed me.

"Ready, sweetheart?"

I muttered a mutinous, *"yes,"* and we hiked the remainder of the loop, the overwhelming majority of which was blessedly downhill. We learned some things about one another on that hike. For example, one of us likes *up*. The other one is me. He learned that when I am struggling, Mr. Positivity needs to hush. I don't do well with external motivation. I learned that I could tell him what I need and have him honor it.

He suggested we drive back to Portland the day before our flight so we wouldn't need to leave as early in the morning. We headed back and at a certain point, it began to dawn on even directionally-challenged me that we did not appear to be headed to Portland. He'd decided to surprise me by taking me back to Cannon Beach for one last night.

Shane had done his research, naturally, and found out that you could get everything you needed to build a fire at the hotel. He hauled kindling, wood, blankets, Adirondack chairs, and coffee down to the deep, wide beach. He brought his bluetooth speaker, and played my favorite music while he stacked the logs. He built the fire the same way he chose the hotel room, the same way he rented the car, the same way he is with me. Meticulous. Thoughtful. Intentional.

The sun set, and Haystack Rock faded into the darkness. We lounged, my head on his chest, wrapped in blankets, and listened to the wistful sound of James Taylor's voice weave in and out of the rhythmic crash of the surf. Up and down the beach, the glow of dozens of fires lit the night, and I had the thought that in that moment there was nowhere else I wanted to be, no one else I wanted to be with, and nothing I would have wanted to change. There was just us. Just me and him, the warmth of the fire, the ocean, the music, and the dark sky.

Chapter Fifteen
Shore

That first summer we were together, Shane talked frequently about going to Block Island. Block Island is off the coast of Rhode Island. I'd never been there, but it was one of his favorite places and he was excited to share it with me. That year, most things were shut down due to COVID-19, but the following summer we planned a getaway.

One sunny July morning, we boarded the first ferry of the day and headed to his island for the weekend. It was a very different experience than going to the island in Maine. No endless planning and packing supplies for the trip. We, along with most of the other passengers, walked on with only our suitcases. There was a fair amount of partying already in progress, despite the early hour. We walked off the boat directly into the downtown area, which teemed with day trippers and drunks. Cars, mopeds, bicycles, pedestrians and baby strollers all jockeyed for position on the narrow streets. It was kind of stressful, actually. Where on the island in Maine I immediately felt at ease, on Block my shoulders tightened initially, disembarking into the chaos.

Shane noticed my reaction and reassured me that just outside of downtown, the pace would be slower. We walked up the hill past inns and restaurants until we reached the end of the road. The hotel came into view. I recognized it from a photo he had framed on his bedroom wall. In the photograph, a huge full moon looms behind the building, but this beautiful summer morning the distinctive red cupola was framed by a bright and cloudless sky. We walked toward the entrance across a sprawling, manicured lawn full of Adirondack chairs overlooking the Atlantic.

The Spring House was built in 1852, and had a long, deep veranda with robin's egg blue ceilings. Its railings were lined with vibrant purple and pink hydrangeas. The funny thing about hydrangeas is that the colors they take on have everything to do with where they're planted. You could take two identical seeds, plant one on one island and one on another, and one might grow to be deep blue, the other one an intense pink, depending on whether the island's soil is acidic or alkaline. I guess in the end, we're all colored by the dirt we grow in.

It's one of those kinds of places where you'd not be completely surprised if a woman in turn-of-the-century clothes glided down the incredible, curved staircase, and if the chairs on the lawn were populated with dandies in straw boaters, they would not have seemed out of place. There was a sense of history there, but not mine. I was pretty sure I'd always feel like a visitor there. Happy to be there, but forever living out of a bag. Never rooted.

Shane has two speeds, ninety miles an hour or reclined on a beach. These are the things you learn over time. Historically, I'd acquiesced to whatever my partner wanted out of an experience and then felt put upon or resentful about it. My idea of vacation is not going at warp speed. I like to be active and do things, but my everyday life and job were fast paced and high stress, and I needed more ease and comfort. We talked about it, and Mr. Energy agreed to slow down a bit. He has a tendency to plow ahead, and can be fairly singular. He'd also functioned alone for a long time. That's the thing with him, though; when I remind him that I am here, too, he stops. He listens. He pivots. He shifts for me.

———

After a full day of sunshine and salt water and walking, we headed back to relax before dinner. I went up to the room to shower and he headed out to enjoy a cigar. Eventually, I joined him on the lawn, content to drink my coffee and eavesdrop on people's conversations, including his. Our regular-life schedules were in opposition. I had a very talk-y, feelings-y job. I communicated and thought and took in people's stories all day, every day. His job was more physical and more solitary, so he spent much of the work-week quiet and alone. So, when it comes to our down time, he wants to talk and I want to… not talk. He liked to be in the thick of things with people, and I was generally all set on the people front. I'm an extrovert, but even we social butterflies have our limits. This sometimes led to him thinking there was something wrong, when really, I was just deeply appreciating solitude or the lack of the sound of my own voice.

A woman sat down in the lawn chair next to him. Shane's a bit of a story magnet, too, as it turns out. She worked on boats and houses and was sharing with him her story of living on an island in the Caribbean for 24 years and how people would come down and, in the grand tradition of colonizers, tried to make it something it's not. They ignored the advice and accumulated historical wisdom of the people who'd been building homes there for centuries. She talked about how the new people flocking to the island eschewed the courtyards, vaulted ceilings, and shuttered windows that work with the island weather in favor of recreating their East Hampton mansions in order to live in tax-break paradise. They tried to assert their will on an island. Having done the research, I can tell you that does not work. Then, when island life was not what they expected– vacation in perpetuity–they were stuck trying to sell a $10 million dollar home on an island that can't support that.

Perhaps that's always the balance that needs to be struck. Perhaps if you have to inflict your will on something to make it yours, it never can be.

We made our way upstairs to dress for dinner. While I was doing my hair, I heard the unmistakable sound of pouring rain and peered out the bathroom window to see all the people we'd just left fleeing the sudden deluge. Moments earlier, there'd not been a cloud in the sky.

Shane was a little concerned because he had a vision for our dinner and wanted me to have a specific experience. By the time we were dressed and downstairs, the rain had ceased. The sun was back out and we were seated at a white wrought iron table nestled up to the railing on the deep porch, which was perched above a salt pond ringed in cattails, with the blue-green ocean beyond.

We ordered our food and talked. About mid-way through our entrees, the sky opened up again, and sheets of rain began pouring down. Some people scattered immediately, requesting tables inside. Some of the more intrepid and intoxicated folks hung in there for a bit, inching their tables back from the weather bit by bit. The gutter was emptying out a few feet from us and it created an impressive spout. I joked that if this were House Hunters it would be referred to as a "water feature."

Almost everyone else fled indoors, but not us. We had a front seat to Mother Nature reminding us of exactly who is in charge. I love storms like that; they make you feel small in the best way. In recovery we call it being right-sized. Eventually, the rain began to ease, and out over the water a gorgeous spectrum of color appeared. It grew wider and taller, and the colors became deeper and richer moment by moment. That's the thing about life, if you can endure the storm, beauty nearly always follows.

The moon began to rise, full and orange. Shane told me it was called a Buck Moon, which relates to the fact that the antlers of male deer reach their peak of growth around this time in July. I Googled it later that evening and apparently, for believers in astrology, this full moon is a source of energy and relates to the abundance and ripeness of summer and to a time of unique personal development. I closed my laptop. I was tired of personal development, and frankly,

Mr. Energy had enough get up and go for the both of us.

Shane's daughter Courtney and her husband Matthew came to join us for one of the days we were there. Courtney and Matthew are pure sunshine. Easy, sweet, and fun to be with. We went down to the dock to wait for their ferry, and soon enough Courtney, petite and beautiful with long, wavy dark hair, dressed in a long gingham sundress and picture hat, and Matthew, tall with broad shoulders, bearded and handsome, disembarked, smiling broadly.

We rented mopeds, and explored the island. We made our way out to Sandy Point, the northernmost tip of the island, which Shane insists looks like a dolphin. It's a long, narrow peninsula of beach with water on both sides. The waves come in from each direction and crash together where the land ends. Shane lay down in the sun and the rest of us walked the beach. Courtney and I chatted about sharks, and how I'd recently discussed with my co-worker Jen that there is an expert in Australia who is trying to re-brand human encounters with sharks as "interactions." Courtney and I laughed at the idea of shark-centered language, and agreed that while sharks shouldn't be vilified, the word interaction seemed a little tepid. We flirted with the pod of seals that came right up to the water's edge. Turns out, Matthew has a thing for seals and insisted on sitting in the shallow water, hoping they'd come nearer. We offered up the very real likelihood that where there are many seals, there is almost definitely something that snacks on seals–and we were somewhat fearful he might have an... interaction of some sort–but he was undeterred.

This part of the island resonated a little more with me, probably because there were very few people, it was mostly ocean and sky. Impossibly tiny piping plovers darted here and there at the water's edge. It was quieter, so we were able to talk more and connect. I'd grown really fond of Courtney and Matthew. I'd resisted it at first, and maybe they had a little, too. I suppose we all had our own previous experiences to move past, and I didn't want to get attached to them only to have things not work out. Bad enough if Shane and

I fell apart. I didn't think I could withstand another onslaught of collateral losses. It was unsuccessful, of course–my plan to remain detached. I'm really not wired for arms' length, in the end.

After a while, we got back on our mopeds and headed back to town. When we saw them off at the ferry after dinner, I found myself a little teary that they were leaving and I suggested that maybe next summer we could plan a trip with them. Shane looked at me and smiled that smile.

On the second full day of the long weekend, we took a cab to the beach. The sun was high and hot, and the sand was just this side of unbearable to walk across. Mr. Meticulous found the perfect spot for the chairs we'd rented, and immediately fell asleep in the sun. Falling asleep on a dime is one of his spiritual gifts. I walked down to the water, which was clear and surprisingly warm. It was neither high tide, nor low; the waves lapped gently on my legs as I waded out a bit. There were big fish darting everywhere. I'd never seen so many at the beach.

Ten-year-old Laura, who was tempted to jump into the big tank at every aquarium she ever visited, would have been in heaven. When I was little, I desperately wanted to be a mermaid and live in the depths of the sea. I could hold my breath for a fairly long time, and I always swam as close to the bottom as I could get in whatever body of water I was in, with my eyes wide open, undeterred by saltwater or chlorine. I loved the way sounds became muted, and the blinding sun became tranquil and silvery. I could still hear the chaos above the surface, but I had the buffer of the cool water to make it all manageable. It felt cozy and safe. The minutes underwater offered a merciful reprieve from a world that felt inherently dangerous and overwhelming. Eventually, I'd feel the need for breath build in my chest and I would reluctantly break through the surface of the water in search of air, flinching at the onslaught of noise and light.

I stood on the edge of one island remembering another. Same

ocean, different shore. I thought back to how someone from James' family had extended an invitation for me to come back and visit the house in Maine, and while the kindness of the offer genuinely touched me, I couldn't. And I knew it immediately. There was no mulling it over, nothing to figure out. Too much had happened. And the reality was, not only couldn't I return, I shouldn't. It was his island, not mine. And it should be. And it wasn't unfair. It just *was*.

I knew that the island I'd loved, the island that held me and fed me and healed me, didn't exist anymore. I knew if I returned, it would not feel the same. Sometimes you can't go home again, even when the welcome mat is still out.

I looked down the beach at a woman about my age, also standing in the water looking out at the horizon. Her face was in shadow, obscured by a broad brimmed sun hat. I wondered if she felt about this island the way I'd felt about mine. I wondered if it called to her when she left, beckoning her back. I wondered if I'd always feel the ache in my chest when I thought back to the rocky shores and rippling meadows in Maine. In a way, I hoped so. The ache had become precious to me. It was mine, even if that small bit of land surrounded by the vast, blue Atlantic wasn't.

If this grief was the cost of having seen the stars hung low on that island, I'd gladly pay it again. I knew I would miss it forever. I also knew I would never go back. I recalled my friend's grace-filled words about her beach house again, and finally truly understood them. I was blessed to have had that beautiful island for the time I did. Some people never get that. Some people go their whole lives without that magic. I couldn't go back, but I finally understood I wasn't losing it. I would always have what the island gave me. Those gifts couldn't be taken away. The beauty. The grief. They were mine. They belonged to me.

My eyes stung as acceptance finally settled on me with all the weight of the ocean. I released the island and sank to my knees, the peaceful rolling swells closing over my head. I opened my eyes and the briny water welcomed my tears home.

———

We woke on the last day to chilly weather and grey skies. Before breakfast was over, the rain had begun. We had a few hours to kill before the ferry. Shane suggested we go shopping, which normally would be right up my alley, but my need for clothing with the words Block Island or references to day drinking on it remained steady at zero, and as it turned out, I didn't want anything ocean-scented or made of shells, either. I did buy Scout a bandana with anchors on it, because, fashion. We darted into storefronts when the rain got more intense, stopped for coffee, and talked about the weekend.

When it came time to get on the ferry, I was happy to have spent the time with him there, but not sad to leave. It was Shane's place. A place I'd happily return to with him, a place we'd surely make new memories–but it didn't call out to me, and I didn't miss it when we left.

My vacation compass seems to be set to home as well. When I think back to vacations I've loved, my reaction has always been *"I could live here."* I guess I have always cared less about an escape from life and more about creating a life I didn't need to escape from.

Chapter Sixteen
Woods

When I was little, I regularly escaped to the woods. My younger sister, my best friend, and I would leave the house first thing in the morning and spend the day exploring, building forts, and racing down the tree lined path to Fresh Pond. When we spent time at our grandmother's house on Cape Cod, our favorite place to play was behind her shed, in a little tangle of wilderness that we divided into rooms to play house. I always felt at home with my feet in the dirt and the leaves overhead.

When I lived in Washington State, the best part of the day was nearly always when I walked my youngest to school on the path through the woods behind our house. We'd hold hands and chat as we made our way through the fern-lined walking trail, stopping to admire banana slugs and mushrooms. We often went on hikes as a family amidst the moss-covered rocks and towering cedars of the Pacific Northwest.

Then I lost that for a while. I went long stretches without losing myself in the woods. Living on the shoreline of Connecticut offered fewer opportunities for hiking and exploring, but I still had opportunities to connect with that part of myself, whether it was on the island in Maine or in the mountains of North Carolina.

For the first few months of my relationship with Shane, there was nothing to do. All of the normal getting-to-know-one-another, date-type activities were unavailable. There was nothing open, people weren't gathering anywhere–no movies to see, no restaurants, no live music. The result of that was that most of our early dates involved what one of us refers to as walks.

On our first date, we took a walk through the woods. There was a beautiful suspension bridge over a fast, shallow river. The bridge is called the Thoreau Bridge and on the handrail is engraved, *"The universe is wider than our views of it."*

On that initial walk we stayed on easy trails and I spent the majority of the time trying to be cute. He'd not met Scout yet, and he seemed less enthralled by all the dogs on the trail than I was. That's crazy to even remember now, because now he and Scout are madly in love, and she has completely taken over his life.

On another early date, he took me on a nice, easy hike at a local state park known for its waterfalls and covered bridge. About halfway through the loop, we came across a fire tower. These structures were built to provide housing and protection for people whose job it was to look out for forest fires. We walked inside and began climbing the stairs. He charged ahead. Of course. I took my time, admiring the stone walls. As I reached the first landing, I saw the word LOVE written in chalk on the wooden riser of one of the steps. At the next landing, the word WINS. I paused for a moment, rolled my eyes at God for being so heavy-handed, and took a photo. Then I walked the remaining flights to the top of the tower, where Shane was waiting for me, smiling that smile. I didn't say anything. It was too early to talk about something as permanent as love, even if it was written in chalk.

Shane's neighborhood backs up to a greenbelt that is home to a series of trails that wind through the woods and alongside a brook that empties into a lake. Once Scout became a participant in our hikes, we frequently walked down the hill and explored the wilderness that is literally his backyard. One early summer afternoon we headed down to let Scout cool off in the water, and as we descended a steep incline down to the trail I spotted a series of cairns on a log, almost out of view. I walked over to see them, and spelled out in twigs on the moss in front of the log were two words.

LOVE WINS.

Once again, I took a photo and then put my phone away, slipped my hand into his, and walked in silence for a bit. *"You okay?"* he asked.

"Yes."

———

At one point, Shane decided Scout needed a new hiking harness–one that had a handle on the back in case he ever needed to rescue her from falling off a cliff. I posited that another super strategy would be not to go on cliffs, but he ordered it anyway. It's hard to know which of them loves hiking more. Now, when she sees me put on my hiking boots and he puts on his pack, she runs in circles in anticipation. When she is chasing chipmunks or trying to dismantle a tree to get at a squirrel, he inevitably remarks that Scout is the perfect name for her.

I smile, because he says it every time.

The trails we took began to be more rugged, and require more of us–because dates and relationships are not the same thing. We talked about life. Ours. The one we were beginning to build together.

We tried to get to the woods at least once a weekend. We had some spots we grew to love, some more challenging than others. There was a pond up in the northern part of the state where we liked to hike and paddleboard. It was more of a walk than a hike, strictly speaking, but it was rugged enough and long enough that it satisfied him and not-UP enough that it appeased me.

Every now and then, though, he'd get a little sneaky. One day, he found a hike that he initially said was listed as moderate. I was instantly suspicious. Moderates are shady as hell. Easy is easy. Difficult is difficult. Moderate is open to interpretation. In the truck on the way there, he conceded that it might actually be *strenuous*. This was highly controversial and I had a lot of feelings about it, but it was a beautiful day so off we went.

The first half was awful. So much up. Up makes me angry. Then there was the summit, which I guess was pretty but I was too winded and grouchy to really appreciate it. We spent a few minutes up there drinking water and enjoying the breeze, and then we continued on the loop downward. The descent was really challenging but fun.

At one point there was a steep crevasse and Shane needed to scrabble down and then lift Scout down. How did he do that? Well, with her harness handle, of course. Scout was not in agreement with this plan. There was a lot of HELL NO from her, but as soon as she was in his arms she was fine, which I deeply understood.

In previous times with previous partners, pets, and situations, I would not have been okay with it. But this was not then. This was me and him and her. This was us. And he is never reckless with us, so we trust him.

Chapter Seventeen
Closets

It was a rainy Wednesday night in August, and I was sitting on the tarmac in Philly, waiting for my flight to depart. Matt's wedding was Friday and I was headed to Cincinnati to be with him. He met his amazing fiancé, Chris, eight months prior, and within weeks they were talking about Matt relocating, and marriage soon thereafter. As I sat there, I had been with Shane for seventeen months.

I had my laptop open to the toast I'd written for Matt's reception. When Matt and Chris started dating, I insisted on a Zoom interview. They met on the heels of one of the hardest times of Matt's life–a period of deep grief. I am somewhat (insanely) protective of Matt, and I wanted to get a sense of who this person was who had so quickly worked his way into my friend's heart. I took this interview VERY seriously. I came prepared with thirteen questions, questions that might have seemed inconsequential–some even silly. They weren't.

The questions ranged from, *"Tell me about a time you made a big mistake and what you learned from it."* to *"Do you believe Matt is the best thing since pizza or are you not particularly bright?"* to, *"How many sweaters is too many sweaters?"* which is obviously a trick question.

His fate hung in the balance of a particularly important litmus test, *"What are your views on Dolly Parton?"* When his response was to burst out laughing, then get super serious and respond thoughtfully, I knew he was special. I logged off and said aloud to no one in particular, *"Matt is going to marry that man."* I knew it.

As I looked over the words I planned to say as my beloved friend married the man of his dreams, I thought about how unpredictable and amazing and hard and weird and devastating and beautiful life is.

The previous week, Shane sent me a text with a photo of one of his closets, which he had emptied for me. His bedroom has two closets, both of which were full of clothes, hung so neatly they could have been an ad for those organizing companies–an ad you would look at and say, *"NO ONE'S closet looks like that."* The text read, *"Surprise… you now have a closet all to yourself."* Followed by, *"If you choose to use it, of course."* I sent the photo to Matt and he immediately inquired, *"Where's the shoe racks?"* I responded, *"That's it. I'm not moving in."* Matt replied, *"That's just the sweetest thing. I'm a big Shane fan."*

That was no small thing,

Shane had been doing things like this for quite some time. Emptying a drawer, and waiting for me to use it. Rearranging his kitchen because he thought it might make it more usable for me, given how much I love to cook. He mentioned wanting to freshen up his bedroom so we looked at paint samples. He brought up wanting to replace the carpet and look at new furniture. I kept responding, *"It's your condo. You do what works for you."*

Don't factor me in.
Don't plan for me.
Yours, not ours.
I'm not falling for this again.
This isn't my home.

This isn't my home.
This isn't my home.
This isn't my home.

My lease on the apartment in New Haven would be up in a few months and a decision of some kind needed to be made. I vacillated between wanting to stay put or perhaps trying to find a place closer to his. I'd spent every weekend for over a year packing up and traveling to him, always in transit, always a little displaced. We'd recently had a conversation about the possibility of living together. It was a topic he'd raised periodically, and one which I typically deflected. He was talking about what we could do to make his place feel comfortable for me.

I insisted that it was *fine*. I was at ease there. When he was there. But if he was going out, or had something to do during the weekend, I didn't want to be there. It was comfortable enough, I guess, but not home–and if I was going to be alone anyway I would rather be in my own space.

For one thing, it was brown. His condo, that is. All brown. And when I say all brown, I mean ALL BROWN. Tan walls, tan carpet, brown sofa, espresso colored wood furniture. Brown, brown, brown, brown. Dark and masculine, immaculate, impeccably organized, but brown.

Don't get me wrong, I like brown. It's lovely. Coffee, for instance, is brown–and coffee and I are a love story for the ages. Some Labrador retrievers are brown. Big fan. A well-toasted bagel? Forget about it. My favorite boots. Scout's eyes. These are all delightful, brown things. And I gravitate toward neutrals–but like… more than one. My apartment in New Haven had white walls and grey and beige and natural wood and metallics. It was airy and bright. And *mine*. I'd collected the things I had – some I'd had for a long time, some I accumulated after my life had been absorbed into someone else's and I'd gotten rid of many of my own things. After I let myself disappear. My apartment felt calm and beautiful and inspiring. It may not have felt like home as I'd always imagined it, but it was mine. I was entitled to be there, no matter what–and that felt safe.

When we talked about potentially living together, when he could actually get me to sit still for that conversation, we both acknowledged it was not the time to buy property together. The housing market had been insane since the pandemic. People were fleeing New York City to the relative safety of Connecticut. Realtors were saying they'd not seen anything like it since 9/11. People from the city snapping up Connecticut properties, sight unseen, for tens of thousands of dollars over the asking price. If we were to move in together it would need to be into his place until prices came back down.

So… me, uprooting my world to make my home with the man in my life. In his space. Not mine. Not ours. His. Logo Togo, redux. Oh, you want me to leave everything behind and make your life my life, your dream my dream, your family my family?

Awesome. Love that journey for me. Again.

That wasn't the way he saw it, of course. But then, he wouldn't. It was his home. He was trying to talk through how it could work to fit me and my stuff into his condo with its oddly-shaped living room and spiral staircase, which was cool but made furniture placement a nightmare. He was talking about the dining room and said, *"I'm not sure your table would fit. It's really nice–I bet you could sell it."*

I love my dining room table. It's got a wooden base and a concrete top. It was the first major purchase I made for my new apartment when James and I broke up. Previously, I'd had a huge, beautiful dining room set from when I was married. It seated ten. Part of the story I was writing for the life we'd lead. I was always planning for the life I was sure we'd have *someday*. The one right around the corner, just out of sight. The life where we entertained and had a house full of family and friends.

Even before I moved in with James, the huge table and chairs resided with him because I lived in a small apartment and he had a big house. When he ended things, I told him I was going to have to sell it and he bought it from me. Come to think of it, maybe the story I imagined for that table *is* being lived and I'm simply not a character in it.

In any case, when Shane made the suggestion I sell my table, tears sprang to my eyes and I fired back immediately, *"I'm not getting rid of ANYTHING."*

Shane looked at me, nodded, and said quietly, *"Okay, sweetheart. You don't have to get rid of anything."*

I went on to say that even if I had to rent a storage unit larger than his actual condo, I was keeping every single thing I owned.

So clearly, all healed up.

Later that night, I thought about a piece of advice I'd given to Matt when he first got involved with Chris. He was still working through some of the aftermath of the demise of his previous relationship, and I counseled, *"Just make sure you're reacting to the person in front of you, not the one behind you."*

Whatever, Laura. Shut your stupid face.

The following Friday, I went straight to Shane's from work. I'd worn a red dress that day, and when I went home at the end of the weekend I accidentally left it behind. Shane had hung it neatly in the newly empty closet. The whole weekend I stayed there and on Sunday, as I was getting ready to leave, he noted that I'd not even opened it to look inside. I felt awful. It meant something to him to have done that and I'd avoided it all weekend.

Before I left, I grabbed my hiking boots (which had moved in with him already) and placed them neatly on the floor in the middle of the closet.

On the drive home, with Scout sitting next to me, I kept thinking about how he was always creating room for me. I'd been so consumed with not making myself small enough to get lost in someone else's life again, I'd missed the fact that he kept making more and more space for me in his.

Matt started making plans to move in with Chris almost right after they began dating. His adorable little house outside

Indianapolis – the one he'd renovated and decorated with such care, the place he'd healed, and fallen in love, and had his heart broken, and fallen in love again – sold in one day. He seemed so sure of his path forward that was taking him to a new city, a new state, a new love, a new life. Every time we talked about these steps he was taking, I wondered if my snail's pace meant something was wrong.

Was I unsure of our love? I didn't think so. I could honestly say that I'd never been loved the way Shane loved me before. And I loved him more every day. It got harder and harder to leave him at the end of the weekend. But as the width and depth of the wound left by the ending of my relationship with James became fully known to me, I wondered about my ability to withstand that kind of loss again. Was I willing to assume the risk that always goes along with love? There is no such thing as complete safety in love. When you love with abandon you make yourself vulnerable.

Matt moved in with Chris and immediately began putting his stamp on the home that would become theirs. When he took me on a tour of the beautiful house, I could see him in it. They were clearly working together to make it theirs. It made me ridiculously happy. I so wanted that for him. I want every good thing for him because he deserves every good thing. It made me remember doing the same when I moved in with James. When we first started dating, his living room looked like a urinal. Yellow sofa, yellow walls. Bit by bit, it became ours. I thought it did, anyway. We chose colors and countertops, we selected tile and hardware. I brought my blue slipper chairs, and my bookcase and we painted the walls a beautiful dove grey. I placed my yellow hand lettered sign across the room. I framed photos, bought throw pillows, and hung art.

And then in twelve words, it was gone.

Shane was not James. Shane was steady and true. And the reality was, I was not me anymore, either. Not a *me* I recognized, anyway. Not the me that had always loved unreservedly and trustingly. She was gone and I didn't know how to get her back or if that was even advisable.

For weeks, but for the red dress and hiking boots, the closet at Shane's remained empty. Which somehow managed to look emptier than if it had actually been empty. But here's the thing, this is what happens when I stay in a hotel: I immediately unpack and hang everything in the closet or put it in the drawers. I stow the suitcase away. I move in and make the space, even if I'm only there for two days, feel like my home.

Yet at Shane's house, a year and a half in, even after he'd given me a drawer and cleared out a closet, I continued to live out of my suitcase. It would remain next to the bed every weekend, with me taking out only what I needed at any given moment. The only clothes I left there were generally for hiking—things I wouldn't need in my REAL life. During all of this, Shane said nothing. He just patiently waited for me to catch up.

We were sitting outdoors at a restaurant one night and the topic of marriage came up. I asked him if he could ever see getting married again and he looked directly at me and said yes, he thought so. He asked me the same question, and I said maybe. What was interesting was that I didn't feel that little frisson of anxiety when I thought about marrying Shane that I felt when I thought about moving in with him. So then I knew that the doubts I had were not about Shane, and I couldn't un-know that.

I kept coming back to the thought that I was not scared by the idea of marrying Shane—although we were nowhere near ready for that. I was scared at the idea of moving in with him. Almost as though that was a greater act of vulnerability than marriage. I no longer felt conflicted about the idea of joining my life with his. I wanted that.

Home is not just where you live. It's so much bigger and deeper than that. It's rooted in our origin stories, and the nature of those stories informs our relationship with the very idea of home.

We were lying in bed one Sunday morning. I was facing the window, watching the breeze blow the white curtains gently. The bedroom windows overlook the woods and the birds called back and forth from one tree to another, greeting the day. It was the tail end of August; the weather was just beginning to turn. Still summer, but the cool mornings signaled the arrival of our second autumn together. Shane had me wrapped in his arms. My poet friend Kate says Shane's arms make her *"a little less gay,"* which always makes me laugh. I thought about packing up and heading back to New Haven at the end of the day. I thought about going another week before laying my head down on the pillow next to his at night.

I didn't want to.

I realized I didn't want to be anywhere else. I wanted to stay more than I wanted to be safe.

I said, *"I think I'm ready. To move in."*

Chapter Eighteen
Shell

When my youngest kid was in elementary school, their science teacher asked them to "babysit" the classroom snails for the summer. There's a reason she asked the kid and not the parent. I can't remember the teacher's name because she is dead to me, obviously.

Anyway, snails are sexpots. I don't know if you know this. It was brand new information for me, too. Unexpected. Okay, strictly speaking that's not true, but as it turns out, a single garden snail can have up to 430 hatchlings after a year. Just a single snail. And we were not 'gifted' with a single snail. No, ma'am. Also, snails are hermaphroditic and can have babies by way of asexual reproduction. So basically, we were given several highly fertile, one-stop-shopping snail baby-making machines, which was fantastic.

Pretty soon a couple of snails became eleventy-billion snails, which we can all agree is several too many snails for one earnest, well-meaning, but easily distractible kiddo to take care of. I will spare you the grim details of what a playroom smells like in July when an enormous passel of snails leave this mortal realm, but it's something along the lines of a seafood compost heap under a sunlamp. See what I did? I said I would spare you and then I didn't. I'm an unreliable narrator, I guess. Anyway, it was not delightful, but that's the way things escargot, sometimes.

Before the great, undisputedly tragic cephalopod demise of 2011, we spent a lot of time marveling at how fascinating it is to be born with the ability to generate your house yourself and carry it around with you. Snails' shells grow along with them, so they keep the same home throughout their life, because they ARE their home.

When I reflect back, it occurs to me that while I deeply mourned the loss of my partners, the deep grief – the abiding grief – was about the sense of a lost home, a lost family, a lost community.

I've seemingly defined myself by my relationships to the people I held as family and the idea of home I've tried to manufacture. Neither of those things is inherently bad, per se. Family, kinship, belonging, have been integral to identity since the beginning of time.

And the idea of home–even house–is important, too. Creating a beautiful, warm, nurturing place to live for you and the ones you love is a worthy endeavor.

But home can't be external, in the end. If it is, it's too easy to have it snatched away or burned to the ground. If *home* is only a place, it can always be dismantled, lost, or stolen.

I'm not a snail. I've been more of a hermit crab, historically. I've assumed homes cast off by others or offered up by those who have them, and I wear them for a while. Sometimes they fit beautifully, and I get to thinking they're mine, that they're meant for me. Problem is, I seem to keep growing, and so inevitably the shell gets too tight, the pain gets too great, and even if I'm willing to live small and hurting, the shell can't withstand it and cracks, leaving me exposed and cold.

In my friend Matt Bays' beautiful book, *Leather and Lace*, he writes:

"Our relationship hadn't created the love I felt for him. I created that. It existed within me. And that made it transferable. All of the love

within me—the capacity to allow myself to belong to someone, to laugh and cry with someone, to suck the marrow out of life—was portable."

Maybe homes are, too. Or the idea of home, anyway. Perhaps home is not a place but a state. Maybe my inability to find a home was really an inability to be one to myself. I'd always been so desperate for home and family that I was willing to compromise everything to hang onto them. I didn't have homes ripped away from me so much as I bent and folded myself to fit into other people's lives, rather than realizing the life or the partner simply didn't fit. Isn't that what women are always encouraged to do? There's a whole industry based on it. The legacy of Dr. Scott and his sparky Spanx-pre-cursor lives on. Better to spend absurd money on undergarments engineered to turn you into the smallest version of yourself, than to wrap yourself in something that allows you to breathe.

I didn't lose those homes. They were never mine. I think about all of the times I set out to create what I thought home was *supposed* to be, but if I'd been more loyal to myself perhaps I'd have known that nothing outside of me can make any place my home.

Chapter Nineteen
Planted

I love having fresh flowers in my home. They're beautiful and the care is simple. You buy them knowing full well they are already dying. You keep them until they are no longer pretty and then you throw them away.

House plants are quite another conversation. A house plant is a relationship.

My amazing colleague Sheila brought me an African violet plant a while back. Sheila is one of the most impressive people I know. I love her so much. She is brilliant and courageous and gorgeous. I frequently think to myself, *"I cannot believe I get to be her friend."* Honestly, it feels like I'm getting away with something. She gave me the beautiful pot with deep purple flowers, and I didn't have the reflexive reaction I used to have when someone would give me a plant. The exasperated, *Super. You're giving me a JOB.* Maybe that's growth, but probably I just really love Sheila.

It's not that I'm ungrateful. It's just… I've always been a killer. House plants. But only 100% of the time. I'm great with plants outside, but bring 'em indoors? I'm like a super-creepy psychopath who sees a beautiful woman and thinks, *"This time will be different. I'll bring her home and we'll have a relationship! I definitely will not kill this one!"*

And then she's dead.

I try. I mean–I really, really do. Historically, though, I have loved my plants to death. Watering, watering, watering, moving them from place to place. Talking to them. Not talking to them. Trying to crack the code of what I can do to get them to thrive in my care.

When I moved into my new place after my relationship with James ended, Mary made me buy some plants. At IKEA. She still maintains that going to IKEA with me is proof positive of her deep and abiding love for me. She was VERY dramatic about the whole experience. While I was looking around for a Flyrgrpstk fainting couch for her, she said, *"You need something alive in this space."* I told her it would not end well. She said, *"They're Jade plants. They're impossible to kill."* Oh, *really.*

Challenge accepted.

She also made me buy a tall spiky plant and a fake palm frond thingy. I felt good about the latter's chances.

She told me to give the Jade plants three ice cubes a week and the spiky thingy seven ice cubes a week and the fake frond zero ice cubes a week, which seemed unkind but life is hard.

Anyway, I liked those highly-specific instructions. No guesswork. Three ice cubes. That's it. I listen to Mary. She knows all the things.

Then my friend Laurie gave me an Amaryllis bulb at Christmas. I thought, *"Great. Now I have to midwife this sucker into growing and THEN kill it."* Which is, like, extra steps. I put it in a box and ignored it for a few weeks figuring it'd self-resolve. Guilt crept in because Laurie is amazing, so I popped it in a pot with some soil, picked a windowsill, threw it a few ice cubes a week and wished it luck.

I would love to say I'd had some revelation at that point, but it was mostly that I was wrecked and just trying to keep my own head above water. I didn't have the energy or bandwidth to worry about or exert my will on these poor plant hostages beyond the simple marching orders I'd been given.

Pick a spot. Give them enough. Take care of yourself. Carry on.

This hands-off kind of love was new to me. It's hard for me to leave things alone when I see someone I love struggling, but struggle isn't a problem in life, it's a part of it. One of the many brilliant things I've heard in the rooms of recovery is this: *Do your part, then STOP.*

I'm always up for doing my part. I can sometimes be *slightly* less awesome at identifying where my part ends. It's also hard for me to let things die. But again, death isn't the end of life, it's a part of it. People, things, relationships have a life cycle. And then they don't.

I stayed in my relationship with James for nearly seven years. I focused on him so intently that I ignored when the relationship ceased to feed me. I watered and fussed and 'advised' and moved him into the sunlight–pretending the relationship was fine–when really, at the end of the day, it just needed to die.

I know that some things need to die. Some things need to die and no amount of resuscitating or help can, or–and this part is important–*should* bring them back. Some things need to die and we need to call it. Time of death: *right now.*

That's just so damned hard and sad and I hate that it's true. I hate giving up on things. I hate giving up on people. On stories. On homes. And it had been a part of my identity for a while. The person who hangs in there, as though that's some kind of badge of honor. At a certain point, it's not loyalty and it sure as hell isn't love, it's just a refusal to bury the dead.

But if I am being rigorously honest, maybe it was less that I couldn't give up on James or us, and more that I had already given up on me. I didn't want to be alone. I didn't really know how to. I have spent the overwhelming majority of my life tied to people who needed me. I didn't know who I'd be if I wasn't responsible for the daily care and watering of another human being, so I settled for being desperately lonely, but with company. And I didn't want to give up on our story, because it was, and in many ways still is, a really beautiful story.

I loved our story. I thought I loved our story too much to let it end, but I failed to remember that not all stories last a lifetime—they're not all supposed to. My grief over losing James' boys was so profound. I thought our story would include me watching them graduate, find their passions, fall in love, maybe become fathers. And I thought anything less than that was not enough. I think I might have been wrong about that. For seven years, I loved them wholeheartedly and unconditionally. They made me laugh and I enjoyed them so much. I was a steady presence in their lives and they knew how I felt about them every single day. None of that is diminished because our story was shorter than the one I thought we were writing. It's enough. The love is enough and it is not gone. As it turns out, it was portable. I get to keep it. It's mine.

Someone gave me a cactus several years ago. It died. Because, yes—not to brag, I can even kill a cactus. Anyway, I did everything it said to do on the plastic instructions dagger thingy that comes with every plant, but it died anyway. Sometimes that happens. Sometimes you do everything right and something dies anyway. It had clearly been spray painted, though, because no matter how dead it was, it stayed bright orange.

Fine by me. Tra-la-la.

The company I worked for had orange in its logo, so I brought the plant to work, where it stayed for nearly three years. Dead. I pretended it was fine. I mean, it was on-brand and required nothing of me, so it was basically perfect.

I've said many times that both my marriage and my long-term relationship with James ended out of the blue, and that's true. Ish. But both times I knew in my bones something either wasn't right or was no longer good for me. I knew. I knew, but I just couldn't let them die. I couldn't let them die, so I worked more hours, did more errands, cleaned more, worked out more, put on more mascara, volunteered more, went to more meetings… stayed busy, busy, busy. I think I knew somewhere deep down inside me, in the place that gets loud when I get quiet, that to stay still would be to know, and to know would require change–and I just wasn't brave enough.

When my marriage was blowing up, I tried to fix everything I thought was wrong with me–on the outside, at least. I starved myself. I bought new, smaller, trendier, cuter clothes. My make-up was perfection. I shot my forehead full of poison to stave off the wrinkles that did not yet exist. I ran on the treadmill like my life depended on it. I cleaned and primped the house until it looked more like a Pottery Barn catalog than a home. Hustle, hustle, hustle. Everything felt out of control, so I controlled me. At least the vessel of me. *Her.* I made her tinier and shinier.

Oh, and drunk. I drank. Every day.

When my relationship with James was waning, it was different in that the control I was attempting to exert wasn't over myself and it was deeply, profoundly rooted in fear. Maybe that's redundant, actually. Control is always rooted in fear because control IS fear.

Both times, I thought I loved the man in my life too much to let it end, but the reality is I didn't love myself enough to want it to be over.

Both times, I let the fear I felt at the prospect of walking away from a life that bore no resemblance to the one that some yet-wild, dormant part of me knew I could have, paralyze me.

Both times, I told myself the grief I felt at the cost of making the decision I knew to be right and true for me was not survivable. That I needed to do anything and everything to avoid that pain.

One midwinter day, I looked at the pot I'd homed the poor Amaryllis bulb in, and I saw a nascent green shoot. I tried not to get too invested and continued on with my pattern of ice cubes and benign neglect. After a week or two, a stalk bearing a luminous white flower graced the window of my apartment.

In my first book I wrote the following line, *"If your old story needs to die for you to heal, let it die."* That was four years ago. Four years ago. I think I maybe even knew then.

But it was a beautiful story. It was on-brand and required nothing of me. Perfect.

It didn't require bravery. It didn't require change. It didn't require growth. It didn't require me to show up as I am. It didn't require me to step fully and completely into the woman I know I was created to be. It didn't require me to be responsible for my own happiness.

Then there was an unexpected storm and I was uprooted. When that happens you either land somewhere you can grow wild and free or you die. Those are the choices.

When I first started moving my stuff to Shane's place, I packed up a box of only brown things and my plants. I joked with him that I was easing into it so as not to freak either one of us out. I walked around the condo trying to imagine my things living here. Trying to imagine *me* living here. When Shane got home that first night after I unpacked the box, he looked at the dining room windowsill that now held those same jade plants Mary'd made me buy at IKEA, which were thriving. He laughed that big laugh of his and said, *"What is happening here? This place is ALIVE!"*

Chapter Twenty
Rock

On a beautiful Saturday in early June, Shane and I made our way out onto a wide jetty behind a yacht club on the Connecticut shoreline. We were there to bear witness to the marriage of my friend Marley and her fiance, Jason. Marley is the best. She is the master of deadpan sarcasm, and pretends to be super cynical, but is actually one of the kindest people I've ever met. She refers to herself as a resentful optimist, which is maybe my favorite thing ever.

Not all weddings are created equal. Sorry, they're just not. There are weddings you attend where there seems to be an additional layer of magic. Matt's wedding was like that, too. In my experience, it's usually because the happiness involved is so hard-won. I've been lucky enough to attend a handful, and always come away with a renewed belief in lasting love and the power that's born of a community coming together to celebrate it. It was a day positively awash in joy, and not just because the bride's dress had pockets.

It was the first wedding Shane and I attended together. We're at the age now when weddings are fewer and farther between in our friend circles. Truly, there were many social firsts we'd not yet maneuvered together, due to the pandemic. Shane would be meeting my work friends for the first time, it was the first time we were throwing dancing into the mix… the stakes were very high. Things had just begun to open up during what we naively thought might be the tail end of the isolation we'd all endured and we were downright giddy at the prospect of fun and connection.

We stood out on the giant flat stones that would serve as their church, surrounded by water and sun and the people who loved them. I really do love weddings–and to attend a wedding during the pandemic was to watch two people insist that while the world might be on fire, love wins, anyway.

It was the shortest wedding ceremony I've ever seen. It was officiated by our friend Carrie, whose hot pink mohawk blazed happily in the afternoon sunshine. I laughed when it was over so quickly, because that's so on-brand for Marley, who is nothing if not direct. The vows were the simplest, most perfect vows I have ever heard. Carrie turned to Jason and said, "Do you, Jason, take Marley *as she is?*" And then, "Do you, Marley, take Jason *as he is?*"

As she is.

As he is.

Not the shined up future version that might be. As you *are*. Not the unblemished, earlier iteration of you. THIS you. The *right now* you. The floor model. Knowing there are dings. Knowing there's some wear and tear. As is. In *this* moment. The exact woman smiling in front of you. The precise man gazing back with such tenderness.

I still cannot remember it without tearing up. It was so intentional and wise and knowing. It was so Marley.

Later that night, the bride and groom danced their first dance, a salsa to an up-tempo version of *Stairway to Heaven*. I'm telling you—it really was a great wedding. Shane and I danced and laughed into the night. We danced and laughed because if we've learned nothing else during these hard few years of the pandemic, life is so fragile and just too short not to seize joy when it comes your way.

At one point in our relationship, Shane and I had a conversation about the nature of love. Our love. There were some things we were trying to navigate. Shane said something about love being unconditional, and I agreed—with a caveat. Love is unconditional; relationships are absolutely not. Relationships have all kinds of conditions. Some are fairly, but not universally, standard—like fidelity and honesty. Some more specific and individual, like rules of engagement, not talking during Project Runway, and not ordering unauthorized anchovies on pizza, which we can all agree is an act of violence. But whatever they are, all healthy relationships have conditions. What are boundaries, if not conditions?

I remember one Sunday when I was going through my divorce, sitting in my seat in church after the service ended. I was weeping inconsolably, and my best friend Angela and our pastor's wife, Jacquie, were trying to comfort me. I sobbed that I didn't know how to stop loving my husband, regardless of what had transpired. I didn't seem to have an off button. How do people do that? Just stop? I felt as though that's what was expected of me, and I knew I wasn't wired for it. It felt as though I couldn't stop loving him and I wasn't allowed to go on loving him, either: stuck between a rock and the hardest, loneliest of places.

It occurs to me that in our marriage vows we promise many things, and none of them are to actually stay married. We say we'll love forever, not be married forever. I mean, that's the earnest hope, of course—but we don't all get that. I'd stood, on another beautiful June day two decades prior, and promised to love, honor, and respect my ex-husband, for all the days of my life.

And here's the thing. I will. I get to. I get to love him forever. I get to choose that. He and I have come back to such a sweet place of genuine affection. Once upon a time, we chose each other. We both had a ton of work to do to get healthy, and we both messed up, in different ways. I couldn't always see that, but I do now. We've grown a lot since then, and earned some wisdom—and now, every so often, I call him on my drive home and we laugh and connect over memories that only the two of us share. We're like fox-hole buddies who have this long, complex history, but really, really love one another.

As is.

—

I remember when I first saw the movie, *The Theory of Everything*. It is a biopic about Stephen Hawking and his wife, Jane. The movie begins with the two of them meeting at Cambridge. Jane, a young woman studying French and Spanish, and Stephen, pursuing his PhD in Cosmology.

Theirs is an unlikely love story. He is an ardent atheist, she is a faithful member of the Church of England. Despite this, they are drawn to one another. She of the arts, he of the sciences. She of the heart, he of the head.

They begin dating, and Stephen starts to experience symptoms of what we now know to be Lou Gehrig's disease. He is given the devastating diagnosis, and told he can expect to live no more than two years.

They are impossibly young. They are in love. Jane persuades him that they should make the most of whatever time they have. They marry, they have children. His physical condition deteriorates but his brilliant mind remains. He gains international recognition for his singular pursuit of a universal theory, one that will essentially explain the whole world–how it came to be, how it will end. Stars and black holes.

As time passes, the toll of caring for her husband and children begins to show on Jane's face. She looks less open and joyful, more stressed and determined. The Jane she thought she would be has been shelved. Stephen, despite his challenges, seems happier than she does–more capable of enjoying life. His professional journey has surpassed any dream he might have had for himself; she's not yet really embarked upon hers. Things are complicated.

Aren't they always?

When the movie came out, Stephen Hawking was 72 years old.

He was diagnosed at 21. He had outlived his initial prognosis by almost half a century.

That's not what Jane signed up for.

It sounds harsh, but it's true. She thought she was only going to have two years with this brilliant, wonderful man that she loved. She knew it would be difficult and heartbreaking. And it was, just in a different way than she expected.

But the thing that struck me, sitting there bearing witness to their story, is that *none* of us gets exactly what we signed up for in this life. That's simply not the way it works. There is always the unforeseeable. People let us down; they break our hearts. They leave too soon; they stay too long. We get hurt. Every single one of us, by someone, at some point. No one escapes this thing unscathed.

There is a point in the movie when Stephen explains black holes. Black holes occur when a star burns through the last of its fuel. Something spectacularly bright and seemingly indestructible collapses in on itself and becomes so heavy, *so* dark that no light can escape, and anything in reach of its gravitational pull is destroyed and consumed by the darkness.

It sort of took my breath away.

At the end of the film I was in tears. Some of it was even about the movie.

Never underestimate the capacity for art to help you heal. This movie allowed for a shift in my heart and in the way I viewed my marriage in the rear view mirror. I think true healing occurs when you can see the whole picture. All of it. The beautiful and the broken, the love and the leaving. Perhaps what healing looks like is all of the truths integrated, so you are no longer idealizing what was or only able to see what wasn't or never will be. The surge of grief I felt when I signed the divorce papers was not more important than the swell of love I felt when he proposed, but it wasn't less important, either.

I sat down after watching the movie and wrote a blog post about it. I wanted to be able to say to my ex-husband what was in my heart; I wanted to try and navigate the seemingly impassable mountains of pain and the uncrossable oceans of grief and say:

"In the end, let's set aside the hurt. Let's set aside the anger, the disappointment, and the heartbreak. Let us put down those dark and heavy things. Let's choose to focus on the things that still shine brightly—these two miraculous human beings that exist because we did. Because once upon a time, before the collapse, before the darkness and destruction—there was an us. Let us stand side by side and marvel at these two amazing creatures who, whether it be by nature or nurture, are made up of bits and pieces of you, and bits and pieces of me.

Your logic, my creativity. Your charm, my way with words. Your drive, my resilience. Your knack for silliness and seizing joyful moments, my desire to connect with people.

Please, God, your sense of direction. Please, God, my sense of occasion.

Our smarts. Our humor. Our curly hair. A little of you, a little of me. A lot of stardust.

Maybe, if I can say anything at all, I will just quote the last line of the movie – uttered by Stephen as he and Jane watch their children run and play,

"Look what we made."

One night, during our last summer together, James and I walked down to the beach at the bottom of the hill for sunset. I sat on the rocks with the dog, and he walked out to the end of the jetty. I took a picture of him from behind. It was a great picture. The sun was setting, and the image of him hovers between silhouette and clarity. His head was somewhat down, and his broad shoulders looked like he was carrying something invisible and heavy. At the time I thought he was simply contemplative, but now I wonder. I wonder what was in his head. I wonder when he knew.

It would be easy to cast him as some sort of villain, but here's the thing: He's not. He was allowed to want something different. He was allowed to stop loving me. There were, arguably, better ways to have gone about it, but maybe it was brave to blow things up if that's the only way he could bring himself to insist on the life he wanted. Because he gets to choose. We all do. Life is just so unbelievably short. There's not enough time to live a life you don't want.

James and I weren't married, but we loved each other. I loved him. We didn't have children, but we raised his sons together for a while. I loved them. We *were* a family. I got to be a part of the lives of those beautiful boys, and I will love them forever, with my whole heart. The fact that it ended the way it did does not negate the beauty of the beginning or the meaning in the middle.

I could finally see all of it.

Chapter Twenty-One
Water

The first summer we were together, Shane decided that I needed to learn to paddleboard. I became a little obsessed. I was nervous at first because I was afraid I would be terrible at it, and for a long time I wouldn't try new things if I didn't think I'd be able to do them perfectly. That impossible standard prevented me from having adventures, finding new passions, pursuing new careers. That fear caused me to live really small for a really long time.

The more I did it, the more I loved it. It seemed to come to me pretty easily. My first time solo, Shane told me I needed to learn how to fall. I very patiently explained to him that I had no intention of falling. He out-patiented me by not responding. What can I say? As my friend Maysha would say, God's still workin' on me.

He's right, of course. It wasn't so much that I needed to practice, so I knew what to do when the unforeseen occurred–although I did. It's more that I needed to approach paddleboarding as a practice. The whole thing is a practice. A practice in balance, in navigation, in endurance, in mindfulness.

Every single important thing in my life is a practice. Some of them have evolved over time, the way rituals do. I do most of them imperfectly, but I try to be consistent. My sobriety is a practice, my faith is a practice. And so is love.

Real love is what you do, not what you feel. I think I used to look at the important things in my life as things to be achieved–like, I got married, and so now I *am* married. I had a child, so I *am* a mother. I got sober, and so now I *am* sober. The truth is, every single one of those is or was a decision I made every day. Or didn't.

Real love is imperfect in its practice, because humans are involved. In my marriage and in my relationship with James I operated out of fear, more often than not. And I think I bought into the idea that making it work was a necessity, and my responsibility– that relationships were carved in stone; stone that needed to be maintained at all costs, so it'd last forever.

———

Anyone who has ever been to a really old cemetery knows that dates and terms of endearment carved into stone and left exposed to the elements, will eventually soften around the edges and fade away. Rock seems hard and people mistake hardness for strength all the time. The fluidity of water might lead us to believe it is less powerful, so if you ask people which element is stronger, lots of people would choose rock. And they'd be wrong. Ask any insurance claims agent:

Water *always* wins.

Water flows over rock, and smoothes out the rough surfaces. The jagged outcroppings of fear are all worn down by its fluid persistence. It may seem like the Grand Canyon contains the Colorado River, but the Colorado River *created* the Grand Canyon. Water sometimes rages and sometimes works patiently, but it always, always wins. And like water, love seeps into the narrowest cracks of the most guarded heart. Over, under, between, and through. Love finds a way. It will prevail against the forces of hardness and resistance, but it can take a long time. It can take an excruciatingly long time.

I looked at love as the bedrock of our lives, and forgot that love isn't something you stand on, it is something you immerse yourself in, drink up, and float on. Love is a force that flows *through* our lives. And even when the love seemingly dries up, in its place are canyons–absences carved out by the mere fact of its presence. And the absences are beautiful, too. No one ever stood at the edge of the Grand Canyon and bemoaned the rock that went missing in its creation.

Love is something you surrender to–which makes perfect sense when you consider that love is the other side of grief, and just like with grief, you can dig in, resist, and try to control yourself in the face of love. Or you can surrender and ride.

———

The first time I went paddleboarding, Shane had me sit on the board and he paddled us around a lake. There I was, leading my best Cleopatra life, getting to enjoy the perks of being out on the board without having to actually do the work. It wasn't terrible. Then he had the audacity to imply that I needed to take the paddle and learn how to do it myself.

He stood in the water and gave me some pointers, while I got my balance and started to figure out how to navigate. Every so often a boat would take a turn in our direction way off in the distance, and cause swells that threatened to knock me off. I learned to crouch, be still, and find my center of gravity again, before I stood back up and resumed.

For a long time, my perfectionism kept me from growing and developing in many areas of my life, including in my relationships. There's nothing more paralyzing than the misplaced, back-breaking belief that you can set being an imperfect human aside. I was afraid to make the wrong decision, I was afraid to be on my own. I was afraid to be honest and vulnerable. I was afraid. All the time.

My friend Samm is an adorable, *terrible*-joke-telling, Applebee's-loving, heavily tattooed, knuckle-headed, surfing sage. Most of her sentences begin with the word "like" and she calls me "dude" more than you might expect. And in between 'like' and 'dude,' she says things like, "*You can't be spiritually shitfaced all the time"* and *"Dude, I'm, like, cautiously stoked."* She's a little Yoda. I remember being in a meeting with her five years ago, before I really knew her. She was emotional about something and said, *"I just really love, like, 75% of the people in this room."* I started laughing so hard I cried, and she has had me laughing ever since. She regularly assures me I'm in her top 3%, which I'm seriously considering adding to my resume. She said once that every morning she has one decision to make, and it is this: Love or fear? How is she going to choose to live today?

I've come to realize that I have to decide. Am I going to live in love or am I going to live in fear? Because despite my ridiculous assertion to Matt all those months ago in that cafe, I do believe in love. I believe in the bravery of BEING in love as an imperfect, wholehearted practice.

When we were done with that first paddleboard adventure, we stood waist deep in the water, on either side of the board. Shane leaned across and kissed me. *"You're a natural, sweetheart!"*

I don't know about that. But I'm finally willing to practice.

Chapter Twenty-Two
Freedom

I've come to realize I don't just fall in love with individuals, I fall in love with families. Lives. Homes. Historically, I would fall in love with the potential of a whole story, of what *could* be. I would be completely invested in a particular ending, and then origami myself to fit into it. And if that relationship didn't have enough space within it to allow me to breathe and grow, I'd simply hold my breath and stay small. *I* did that.

I think for a long time I held the other person in those relationships accountable for that fact, but the reality is that I never insisted on breathing. I never demanded room to grow. And I never allowed for the possibility that it might just not be the right relationship for me, or that I might need a new home. I think there's a difference between commitment and steadfastness, and a refusal to admit that you've either made a mistake or the relationship has run its course. I always thought that if a partnership stopped meeting my needs, or never did, it was my responsibility to get those needs met another way or to pretend they didn't exist.

If home is where you are able to exhale and be known and loved for exactly who you are, then perhaps I've never lost a home. And maybe, just maybe, those elements of home are, in fact, portable. Maybe the moment when you love yourself enough to insist on those things is the moment you find the home you've always longed for. Maybe home *is* something you carry in your heart, after all. God damn it.

When I left James' house and took that sign from what used to be our living room, I considered throwing it away. I was undone and overwhelmed and it felt like a lie. It felt cruel, honestly. Like a bad joke.

Here's what I've come to believe: Love does win. The long game. Love wins the long game. It just always, always wins. New relationship, no relationship, hard relationship, broken relationship, ending relationship. In the long game, love fucking wins.

The thing about love winning is that it frequently does not look the way we think it will. I believed love winning would look like me being with James for the rest of my life. He was my favorite. I really believed we would make it, but no amount of wanting that to be true could make it so, and that's okay. It was a love I thought would last forever, and here's the thing: it will. It will last forever.

Love is like energy, it cannot be destroyed—only transformed—and it is not diminished by the transformation. Even in the midst of pain and loss and endings, love shows up in safe harbors and offers of help. Love shows up in friends bringing you coffee and sitting silently alongside you in grief. Love shows up in circles of truth-tellers, on hikes, in dogs, and in two people taking a chance on one another. Love shows up in self-care and generosity and sobriety and forgiveness and acceptance.

Love wins. Every time. I believe it. Still. That's the hill I'll die on. I get to choose and I choose love, whatever the hell that looks like.

Hanging that yellow sign was the first thing I did in my city apartment when I moved in. Love seemed like a good starting point. When I was taking things down off the walls as I packed to move in with Shane, I considered what to do with it. I wasn't sure I needed it any more, maybe because I finally believed it. I didn't need its bravado, because I was prepared to be brave.

I found that I was not as worried as I thought I would be. I set out to write this book not knowing where I would be when it ended. What room would I be in, what would my address be? Would I be with Shane? Would I be alone again? Where would home be?

———

I sat in the early morning light on the couch with Scout curled up next to me. Shane was asleep in the next room. The brown condo had become a little less brown. It was beginning to feel like ours. We had done a lot of work to make it so, and I am not talking about paint–although, thank you, Jesus, for new paint.

Shane has told me in a million ways, on hundreds and hundreds of days, that he chooses me. And more importantly, so do I. I choose him, too. And so does he. We choose ourselves and we choose each other. As it turns out, you don't have to do one or the other. We're both completely capable of being on our own–we just want to be together. As we are. At the end of the day, I drive straight home. I can't wait to walk in the door.

I love being with him. I don't have to be. I want to make this work, but I don't have to.

I have to be with me.

I worried so much about finding home and coming home, not realizing that I needed to *be* home. I needed to get sober and go to therapy and walk in the woods and write my way through it. I needed to look back, not to hang on to the past but to learn from it. I needed to forgive, starting with myself. I needed to talk to my friends to work through what my non-negotiables were, and I needed to figure out what I needed in a partner and not just focus on what I needed to *be* as a partner. I needed to honor my needs and give voice to my wants in order to have a relationship that could ultimately work. I needed to be brave enough to try again knowing the risk that goes along with that. *Assuming* the risk that goes along with that.

Because the thing is, this might not work. We might both try really hard and love each other a lot, and it still could go sideways. We both know that. We both know who we are and what we want, and we know there is no guarantee.

We make homes with other people, and sometimes *of* other people, and that either goes the distance or it does not. When something ends, it can be difficult in the face of such disappointment not to paint the entirety of a relationship with a very broad brush. But nothing and no one is all one thing. Just because something ends badly doesn't mean it wasn't ever good.

I don't regret any of the homes I've had or tried to make. Perhaps I've always guessed at what home is or should be, but as any teacher worth their salt will tell you, guessing is not the opposite of learning, it is a part of it. I have come to learn that for me, home is peace. Home is acceptance and presence. Home is warmth and comfort. Home is love. Home is where I breathe easy. It's where I feel able to be my whole self, and to have that self grow and change, and have home grow with me. Home is where history and my story intersect and become something new. Home is where I want to be at the end of the day.

I used to think that home was where your life was contained and safe, but now I believe that, ultimately, home is what frees you. And freedom isn't safe.

And just like that, I'm home.

Not because I've found my home or I've made a new home. *I'm* home. Me. The one thing that can't be taken from me unless I do it myself. *I* am my non-negotiable. Everyone and everything else is a variable. I am the constant. If I live in love and insist on peace, if I accept myself and stay present for my life, I am home. I am *already* home.

Epilogue

It would be easy to view this as a fairy tale ending, but it's as much a beginning and a middle as it is the finish line. I remember hearing Tom Hanks respond to someone who wanted a *Sleepless in Seattle* sequel by saying something like, *What do you want, to see them brushing their teeth? After that it's just life!* He, while being a straight up national treasure, was both right and wrong about that. Yes, at a certain point the initial infatuation and rush of early love settles into actual life, but actual life is where we actually live, and love is a verb, not a feeling.

In this fairy tale midpoint, two people in their fifties (one just *barely*, the other *solidly*) both with rich, hard, and complicated histories are making the decision to choose themselves and each other, and be home. Together.

The first week after I moved in was tough. We found ourselves at odds several times, being short with one another, being ungenerous in our assumptions. Not like us. He has lived alone for the overwhelming majority of his adult life, and I pretty much never have. He is used to doing what he wants to do when he wants to do it, and I am used to compromising and yielding far more often than I should. He is having to learn to bend and I am having to learn to stand firm.

That Friday, I had a really difficult day—one that churned up a lot of fear, and neither of us was handling it particularly well. The following morning we had an argument. We both retreated to our corners. I texted Matt and fed the dog. I did some writing. Mary called and we had a conversation while I did my hair and put on makeup. I washed some dishes and unpacked some more things. Shane came into the room when I was making the bed. When I finished, he wrapped his arms around me. We stood there for a long time.

"Let's go apple picking."

"Okay," I replied, my face buried in his neck.

We said goodbye to Scout, got into his spotless sports car, and drove to the country on a perfect October day. The sun was out and there was just a hint of chill in the air—the kind of day when you excitedly wear a sweater, only to regret it as the temperature steadily rises. He talked a little. I was quiet. At lunch, we reflected on the past few days and what had been hard and what we could do better. There were a couple of bees dive bombing my head, so Shane carefully poured a little of his birch beer onto a plate, to draw them away from me.

We drove up to the orchard. He asked what apples I wanted to pick and I said Honey Crisp and Macoun. He asked if pies were in his future.

I said yes.

As we picked apples, we talked about projects around the house, our kids, what apples are trash (Red Delicious) and work and fear and faith. We walked past a young family taking photos in the orchard. Their little girl looked perfectly at home sitting at the base of a tree, with a small apple clasped in her tiny hands, giggling at her parents' silly antics behind the photographer. Shane and I laughed as we walked past. *"Remember those days?"* he asked.

"I do." I remember those days.

Eventually our bushel bag was full. We walked back through the rows of trees, laden with fruit in varying stages of ripeness. There seemed to be as many apples on the ground as there were amongst the branches. Piles of apples lay in drifts beneath the trees where they started off as flowers on branches that would eventually hang heavy with fruit. Some of them were half-rotten, some seemingly perfect. Why certain apples make it into the bag and others never do is a mystery. I used to feel sort of bad about that; it always seemed like such a waste.

Now I know those apples serve a purpose, too. They may not have been exactly what someone was looking for, whether that's because they were bruised or damaged in some way, they weren't ready, or they fell to the ground simply because some things just do that. They fall–but they're an important part of the cycle, anyway. They oxidize and decay over time. What once was shiny and ripe becomes withered and ugly. That can make it hard to remember it once held the promise of sweetness and sustenance. But a dying apple is still an apple. It still contains everything that made it beautiful and nourishing at one point. It just looks different, is all. The fallen fruit breaks down to its essential elements and readies the soil for what comes next. The remains of the old are the foundation of the new.

We began to make our way back up the path. Shane's phone rang. It was his son. He looked at me. "*Take it*," I said. He answered the phone. I slowed my pace and fell behind. I looked up at the tree-covered hills, at thousands upon thousands of brilliant leaves dying beautifully. Soon it would be winter, and those leaves would lie beneath a carpet of snow, readying the ground for the new growth of spring. Then, as the days warmed and the ground thawed, the water from the melting snow would give life to shoots of green valiantly pushing up through the fecund soil. Beauty would be born from decay.

Because life goes on.

I listened to the comforting sound of Shane's deep voice as he encouraged and advised. I smiled and turned my face up to the sun, grateful for the light and warmth. As we reached the end of the row,

he turned back and mouthed to me,
 "Home?
 "Yes."

~ ~ The Middle ~ ~

Acknowledgements

To Samuel. My sun. My universe had no center until you. Everything got warmer and brighter and better the day you were born. You remain the greatest gift of my life. I love you. To Lily. What a miracle you are. I'm so proud to have you as a daughter-in-law.

To Em. I will leave a light on. Forever.

To my mother. I can see all of it now. I love you.

To Aimee. You are an incredible writer and editor, and an even better sister. Thank you for Ghiorse-ing all over this manuscript, and for being a constant. I don't know anyone smarter or more generous of spirit than you. I love you so much, svaester.

To Stephanie. We'll find our way. I love you.

To Mary. Thank you for taking such good care of me when it was all I could do to put one foot in front of the other. And thank you for believing in my ability to grow something beautiful and new. You were right. And I should never have made you go to IKEA. I see that now. We've made up for a lot of lost time, these past eight years. Let's keep doing that. Your hand in mine, forever- but especially at the Yale Art Gallery, because you cannot be trusted. Love you more than pizza.

To Johnny Sunshine. I'm so glad I ordered you to be my friend.

Thank you for complying. Thank you for your enormous heart, your unfailing kindness, and for the best road trips ever. And to Danny. We miss you, but only every single day.

To Angela. No matter the physical distance, you are *always* in my heart. You're a north star. I thank God for that day at the kindergarten bus stop.

To Laurie. Thank you for my life. To Barbara and Leo. Thank you for providing me with a safe harbor in which to heal. To Judy. Thank you for your treachery and your intuition. To Brady. Thank you for your unending kindness. You are such a good man. To Samm. Top 3%. Easily. Shabon, Elizabeth, Kim, Maysha, Connie, Tina, Martha, Suzanne… The list is endless. It's an embarrassment of riches. Everyone should have a safety net of badasses like you. And to our sweet Izzie. I wish you were here to talk about the book. I know you'd have questions. And a salad. And hydrangeas. We miss you.

To my church-basement, beach circle crew. You are the reason I am here.

To Sheila D. Coleman. There may come a day when I don't feel like I'm getting away with something by getting to be your friend, but today is not that day. You are a profound blessing in my life. Let's change the world, shall we?

To Erin. I took them off the shelf, and look what happened. There is no one kinder, braver, or truer than you. We none of us deserve you, but here we are. And we have Kevin, so there's that.

To Shelley. Ride or die, sister. Thank you for seeing me. #lifer

Daneen, Jen, Laura, Marley, Libby, Jennel, Rachael, Stacie, Steve, Zach, Ted, Mike, Keith, Faith, Sara, Jean, The Sarahs, Ethan, Junette, Rich, Aileen, Christina, Corey, my Family folks and the rest of my work family. I get paid to spend time with people I would pay to spend time with. I am the luckiest.

To Tim. My co-rememberer. It's the sweetest of full circles. On your side and in your corner forever, because we said so.

To Courtney and Matthew. You make everything more fun

and sweet, and I love you both. I feel so lucky to have you in my life.

To Littlest and Thing One. You remain some of the sweetest chapters in my story, and I will love you every day of my life. You were the best bonuses. And to the extended family I was lucky enough to be a part of for a while. Thank you for welcoming me and loving me. I will always be grateful for having walked alongside you for the time that I did.

To Brian Stauffer for his gorgeous cover design. To Lenora Rand for her generosity in letting me use the lyrics to one of my favorite songs, *Lovely Needy People.* You are both examples of the good things that can come of relentless fan-girling. To Lorna Reid, for her beautiful work on the design of this book's interior. I never really noticed formatting before, but I will now- and I'll likely think, 'they should have called Lorna.'

To Juliana Miner for early and helpful feedback. You are the funniest and loveliest. I loved sitting across the table from you trading chapters. Your unofficial endorsement is, maybe, the best thing ever, and it was all I could do not to put it on the front of the book. To Meghan Jarvis Riordan. You ask the best damned questions. I'm in love with your brain, and also your heart. To Glennon Doyle, thank you for, well, all the things. Thanks for getting my ass out of the Subaru and into the church basement—you were a map and a flashlight and I love you so much. To Jen Hatmaker. It's hard to convey what you mean to me, but I guess I'll keep trying. Your heart is the eighth wonder of the world. More of a lighthouse than a spotlight, as it turns out. To Rachel Macy Stafford. You are the most generous, encouraging, and tender person. Thank you for all of your support, and for my mantra. Only Love Today.

To Jessica Faith Kantrowitz, Kate Mapother, and Matt Bays—thank you for the feedback, support, and friendship—and for the funniest text thread in the history of text threads. Writers are the best people. Fight me. Jessica, the coffee pot is overflowing forever. When I start to get cynical about the world, I remind myself there is a Jessica Faith Kantrowitz and I feel more hopeful. Kate—you are so freaking brave. Wait 'til the world gets a load of your poetry. You walk through life with your heart fully exposed. It's astonishing. I'm so glad to call you friend. Also, I was right. I will just sit here in my rightness.

And speaking of Matt Bays. MattBays. My brother. You were with me every single step of the way as I lived this story and wrote my way through it. During the hardest times, you sat outside the dark rooms I was in, singing to me from the hallway so I could find my way back out. Thank you for making me laugh when I didn't think it was possible and cry when I didn't think it was necessary. Thank you for the most gorgeous foreword in the history of forewords. If I were to enumerate the ways in which you make my life better, this acknowledgement would be longer than the murder list. Which is lengthy and 100% exists. Also, thank you for marrying Chris.

Speaking of Chris. Thank you for answering the Dolly Parton question correctly. Otherwise we might never have married you, and that would be tragic because you are a dream come true.

To Scout. One of us was a rescue. The other one is you. Thank you, my sweet, funny, weird, little criminal. You make every single thing better. Except Zoom calls.

To Shane. I'm typing this sitting next to you on the couch. Well, Scout is next to you, but she let me sit on the couch, too, which I appreciate. You're watching golf. On TV. On purpose. Project Runway is more of a sport, but whatever. On a bright March morning two years ago today, we went on our first date. Two years is a hell of a lot of days. Your smile still makes me a little weak in the knees and your arms still make Kate a little less gay. Thank you for peace, laughter, and adventure. Thank you for always having my back. Thank you for perfect coffee in the morning and music on the deck at night. Thank you for your love and patience as I wandered my way home. Water over Rock.

Love won.

Citations

Kantrowitz, Jessica. *The Long Night: Readings and Stories to Help You through Depression*. Minneapolis, NY: Augsburg Fortress Publishers, 2020

Clement, Douglas P. "The 'Revealing' Story of Corsets in Connecticut, a New Haven Tale." CT Insider. CTInsider, September 25, 2013.
https://www.ctinsider.com/connecticutmagazine/home-living/article/The-Revealing-Story-of-Corsets-in-Connecticut-17039992.php.

"Hiraeth Definition and Meaning." Collins Dictionary, 2022.
https://www.collinsdictionary.com/us/dictionary/english/hiraet
h#:~:text=hiraeth%20in%20British%20English,which%20can
%20never%20be%20revisited.

Frost, Robert. *Collected Poems, Prose & Plays*. New York, NY: Library of America, 1995.

The Many, "Lovely, Needy People," recorded 2017, track #4 on *All Belong Here*, June 30, 2017; lyrics used with permission of The Many.

King, Heather. Parched: A Memoir. New York, NY: New American Library, 2006.

van der Kolk, Bessel A. *The Body Keeps the Score: Brain, Mind, and Body in the Healing of Trauma.* New York, NY: Penguin Books, 2015.

Bays, Matt. *Leather and Lace: A Gay Man, Lost Love, and a Road Trip with His Dead Sister.* Cincinnati, OH: Matt Bays, 2022.

Parrott Perry, Laura. *She Wrote It Down: How a Secret-Keeper Became a Storyteller.* Lexington, KY: Laura Parrott Perry, 2017.

Parrott Perry, Laura. "Stardust" Laura Parrott Perry, December 2, 2014. https://lauraparrottperry.com/stardust/.

About the Author

Laura Parrott Perry is a writer and speaker on the topics of trauma, story, addiction and recovery. She is in recovery from alcohol addiction, disordered eating, and childhood sexual abuse. All the things. She is co-founder and CEO of the non-profit, Say It, Survivor, which is dedicated to helping survivors reclaim their stories as a part of the path to healing. Laura also works as a leadership trainer and as a freelance writer for non-profit organizations. She lives in Connecticut, where she has apparently become a hiker. She is frequently found in the woods with her love and their gorgeous reprobate of a dog, Scout.

Made in the USA
Columbia, SC
22 January 2024

30815042R00102